A
VERY
CAPABLE
LIFE

THE AUTOBIOGRAPHY OF

ZARAH PETRI

OUR LIVES: DIARY, MEMOIR, AND LETTERS
Series Editor: Janice Dickin

OUR LIVES aims at both student and general readership. Today's students, living in a world of blogs, understand that there is much to be learned from the everyday lives of everyday people. *Our Lives* seeks to make available previously unheard voices from the past and present. Social history in general contests the construction of history as the story of elites and the act of making available the lives of everyday people, as seen by themselves, subverts even further the contentions of social historiography. At the same time, *Our Lives* aims to make available books that are good reads. General readers are guaranteed quality, provided with introductions that they can use to contextualize material and are given a glimpse of other works they might want to look at. It is not usual for university presses to provide this type of primary material. Athabasca University considers provision of this sort of material as important to its role as Canada's Open University.

A Very Capable Life

THE AUTOBIOGRAPHY OF ZARAH PETRI

JOHN LEIGH WALTERS

AU PRESS
Athabasca University

Our Lives: Diary, Memoir, and Letters

© 2010 John Leigh Walters
Published by AU Press, Athabasca University
1200, 10011 – 109 Street
Edmonton, AB T5J 3S8

Library and Archives Canada Cataloguing in Publication

Walters, John Leigh, 1933–
A very capable life : the autobiography of Zarah Petri /
John Leigh Walters.
(Our Lives: Diary, Memoir, and Letters series)
Also available in electronic format (978-1-897425-42-8)
ISBN 978-1-897425-41-1

1. Petri, Zarah. 2. Hungarian Canadians--Biography.
3. Immigrants--Canada--Biography. I. Title. II. Series: Our lives: diary, memoir,
   and letters (Edmonton, Alta.)
FC106.H95W34 2010   971'.004945110092   C2009-905091-9

ISSN 1921-6653 Our Lives: Diary, Memoir, and Letters Series (Print)
ISSN 1921-6661 Our Lives: Diary, Memoir, and Letters Series (Online)

Printed and bound in Canada by AGMV Marquis.
Cover, layout, and book design by Honey Mae Caffin, intertextual.ca
Cover photograph: Private Family Collection

Please contact AU Press, Athabasca University at aupress@athabascau.ca for
permission beyond the usage outlined in the Creative Commons license.

For Jacquelynn Ann Barnes
Fifty years and still not enough

Introduction

A Very Capable Life: The Autobiography of Zarah Petri by John Leigh Walters is a remarkable book, seemingly straightforward, and highly accessible on one level, yet complex and provocative on another. Walters's purpose in creating this memoir seems simple enough: to tell his mother's life story in a way that evokes her own voice as accurately as is possible. Of course, the memoir genre is not a simple one, and in fact readers may well discern several more nuanced and overlapping purposes behind the manuscript: to tell a woman's story, an immigrant's story, a working class person's story, an elderly person's story, and in so doing, not only to valorize each of these subject positions, but also to reveal his mother, someone who has occupied all of these seemingly marginal spaces, as a truly extraordinary person, one who deserves to be remembered for her place in history as well as for her remarkable personal qualities. Given the range of territories through which it moves, this book will interest diverse readers, from specialists in such areas as women's history, life writing, immigration history, and working class history, to those who simply enjoy a good read.

Readers familiar with the broad story of the immigration to Canada from central and eastern Europe in the late nineteenth and early twentieth centuries, and in particular, with the story of Hungarian immigration, will find in this memoir a compelling case study. While clearly propelled by her distinctive personality, Zarah's story is nevertheless quite representative of the "Hungarian immigrant story," in terms of the factors that "pushed" her family out of Hungary and "pulled" them to Canada, the period of their immigration, the places where they settled, even the problems of adjustment that they experienced. Historians of immigration generally, and of immigration to Canada and from Hungary in particular, will find this book a fascinating and valuable addition to the various primary and secondary sources that evidence/explore the second major wave of European immigrants to Canada in the inter-war years, the more so because it is about a woman, and immigration history in Canada has often been skewed toward a male perspective. Similarly, since women's history in Canada has arguably been biased toward the Anglophone and Francophone majorities, this book makes a valuable contribution to our knowledge and appreciation of the diverse experiences of women who have helped to build this country.

Readers will find here an intricate piece of storytelling, one that offers a skilful rendering of Zarah Petri's lively voice, as she tells her life story, more or less chronological, complete with engaging flashbacks and flash-forwards that lend the narrative coherence and momentum. However, the narrator's voice/point of view is a complicated one, because it is retrospective and thus at once encompasses both the child (or young adult, for example) and the elderly woman, while also at times including the voice of John, the second son, the actual writer, his mother's scribe. Some readers will undoubtedly find such a "memoir" problematic, if not downright objectionable. After all, the voice we hear is not really that of the woman supposedly at the centre of this narrative, but rather, that of the man who dares to speak for her. However, I hope that more readers will applaud Walters's arguably audacious appropriation as a loving act, one that honours his mother by telling her story as authentically as possible rather than allowing it to fade into oblivion, lost, like most such "ordinary" stories, to all but her immediate family, and eventually even to them.

Clearly, readers of this memoir are in the hands of two storytellers, who simultaneously lead them through Zarah Petri's extra/ordinary life. Thankfully, both are artful weavers, and together they re-create the complex textures of Zarah's experiences—the irony, the comedy, and the tragedy that constitute her difficult yet richly eventful life. The narrator takes readers from her childhood in the early years of the twentieth century in the small Hungarian town of Becse, where she and her brother and sisters are left on the eve of the Great War in the capable and loving hands of their grandparents, while their less sensible parents follow the "Judas goat" Count Esterhazy to the wilds of Western Canada in search of a new life there for their young family; to her in many ways ill-fated journey to Ontario, where her poet father has purchased a beautiful but impractical farmhouse, in which later, unable to cope with mounting debts, he commits suicide, leaving his only marginally more capable wife to raise their young family in a foreign land; then to Zarah's marriage as a teenager to John, a fellow immigrant, but somewhat less than kindred spirit; to their struggles during the Great Depression as they raise their two, and later, three, boys; through her challenges as a mature woman, as a widow, and then as an elderly woman confronting the indignities of Alzheimer's disease. Her free spirit and sharp intelligence animate the narrative at every turn, making it the kind of story that once begun, one is loath to leave unfinished. Readers will not soon forget the expressive, albeit at times ungrammatical, voice of Zarah Petri—a woman whose courageous spirit, generous heart, and fierce independence as she confronts whatever challenges fate conjures make her worthy of our attention and respect, as she beckons us to join her in discovering anew the country to which she journeyed so many years ago.

TAMARA PALMER SEILER
University of Calgary

Preface

THERE IS NOTHING ORDINARY, HERE. ARRIVING AS A CHILD from Europe in the 1920s, Zarah Petri marries at age sixteen, and is subsequently released from her job in a knitting mill. ("No married ladies, please.") These are also the Prohibition years, so the young bride confined now to the kitchen, moves to replace the missing income by making and selling "grappa," a homemade liquor, a sweet and satisfying distillate, a quick seller to area speakeasy patrons. Zarah's grappa becomes unexpectedly popular. Zarah prospers, and her missing income is made bigger by twice. Later, during WWII, faced with a heavy mortgage on a farm she bought, between rows of field corn she grows rows of illegal poppies, the seeds of which she sells to the ethnic baking trade to be used in sweet goods. Historical: The federal government of the day forbade the growing of poppies believing it would lead to the manufacture of heroin as it had in China in the 1930s. And through the war when meat is rationed, Zarah markets freshly butchered hogs from the trunk of a car, in the dark of the night, to a thankful Italian and Portuguese public. All these things are punishable by jail time, but she does them anyway. Zarah has her own test for what is proper or improper, taken from the Good Book, Exodus 20: 1–17 saying, "If it is not forbidden here, it is forbidden nowhere." Proof to her purpose, there is nothing in the Ten Commandments about distillates, poppies, or pork.

In the pages of this book I am the son mentioned. My birth occurred during the Depression; no money changed hands on that occasion; the attending physician, Dr. Leigh C. Vanderburgh, was paid for his services by means of two imperial gallons of clear grappa. My middle given name is his.

I am also the writer of the text, carefully presented in the unique way Zarah Petri speaks. All events are true, but because of the character of some of those events the names of several family members have been changed.

JOHN LEIGH WALTERS

"Where have you been?"
"Nowhere."
"What did you do?"
"Nothing."

THE SMALL VILLAGE OF BECSE, PLACE OF MY BIRTH, IS IN THE best part of Hungary I think, the southern part where spring comes early and fall lasts late into the year, just a little snow and the fruit of the mulberry trees in early summer having the taste of sugar, and as big as your thumb. I love this place, every inch of it. Many families in my village talk of leaving, some preferring to go to the United States passing through Ellis Island in New York, or some choosing Canada passing through Halifax Harbour, to seek a new chance away from the war, so they said, but that is just an excuse because our town of Becse in Hungary is not affected by the war, our town being so minor. Who of importance would want to come to Becse? None.

The town's men are especially excited at the idea of leaving for what they are calling the New World. The women a little more wary, women being always a little more wary than men, because of childbirth. My grandmother, my Oma, the smartest person I have known in my life, then as now, hearing of all these big stories of success in the New World, a logical thinker was she, saying that many who leave Becse will taste bitter bread, the way she would describe it, later proving to be correct. I will draw for you the design of my Hungarian village. It looked like this, with all the farms shaped like a slice of pie and the houses at the tip, if you saw it from the sky:

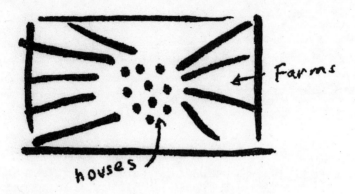

Houses and farms in Becse. Credit: J.T. Cawllender.

That's how it was done at that time. There was wisdom in this. Even as a child I thought this was a smart way to build a town. This was a town located in the country, giving everyone living there the best of both town and country. Each of the farms about twenty acres, cut in these pie shapes so that all the houses are close to each other at the point of the slices, providing close neighbours to help each other, a popular requirement since money wasn't much in use. All neighbours had a reliance on each other in the farm harvest, passing out help whenever asked for, doing so in lieu of actual cash and helping anyone who asked, building up a personal account of good will, much as a bank account but this one being real, being help when it is needed. So, none felt poor or insecure, two of the most important things in life.

But it is asked, how come so many Hungarians from the village of Becse left for Canada and fewer to the United States by proportion? Well, many went to Pittsburgh in the great state of Pennsylvania, everyone knows that, even a famous son of such playing football, the surname Namath being common to Becse, Joe too is everywhere.

So, you ask in repeat: how did it happen that so many Hungarians went to Canada and something fewer to Pittsburgh by proportion? Well, I would say one man is responsible, and he is Count Paul Oscar Esterhazy and he was doing such for improper reasons. He was what is called a Judas goat. A Judas goat is one which is trained at the abattoir to lead the sheep to slaughter, all the foolish sheep following the goat, thinking the goat appears knowledgeable, seems to be okay, nothing bad going on in here, come on let's go. In a similar way Hungarian families followed Count Paul Oscar Esterhazy.

Here is what happened: The Count advertised by post office billing boards the chance for families to leave Hungary and go to the province of Saskatchewan in the country of Canada, where they would surely prosper. The land is so rich he said, that the corn grew to the sky, the rivers so thick with fish you could scoop them up by hand. There would be opportunities to earn real money he said, not just trading farm goods for hard goods as in Becse, but putting real cash in the pocket. All the men in town believed what the Count claimed, wanting to believe the Count's story because men like to go adventuring and here was their chance with the Count, not knowing the Count was speaking truthlessly. To explain further, Count Paul Oscar was born to the wealthiest family in Hungary. Being rich, well he must also be smart and that was the general feeling about rich people at the time. Well, we all know much better now, some of the dumbest people in the world being also the richest. And you can just put the Count in there.

But I am calling him a Judas goat because these are the only words to suitably describe him, influencing the men of small towns, breaking up families. Imagine, when I was just nine years old I was required to wave goodbye to my mother and father as the steam train pulled out from our little town in Hungary, my mother and father waving out the window back to us, leaving their four children behind, promising someday later to return for us.

So, we were left behind in the care of my mother's mother, she being my Oma, who was already getting old and tired and her husband, my Opa, who had but one leg remaining. Just one, the other being run over by a breakaway wagon, and his crushed leg is amputated off with no anaesthesia, just a cup of brandy, the town's veterinarian cutting through his limb, two other men holding him down because of the pain of it, right before my eyes, using turpentine as a medicament to cleanse it, producing even more pain, making my grandfather, lying in the grass, to flail his arms and scream like an infant. Months later he took me aside to apologize for his behaviour, an apology not required since there is just a cup of brandy and a cloth tourniquet twisted tight to cut off the blood circulation, to reduce the pain and to keep from bleeding to death.

The Count advertised throughout the country, and the townsmen of Becse, my beautiful Hungarian village, bought the biscuit so as to speak, the Count saying he has successfully built a new Hungarian town in the province of Saskatchewan, which he claimed is even better than Pittsburgh. And he named the new town after himself, calling it Esterhazy, by his family name out of improper proudness, I think. It is still on the map of Canada if you look at the province of Saskatchewan, to the eastern part near the Manitoba border you can still see Esterhazy, the town started by the Count, who said by bringing Hungarian families to Esterhazy, he would be bringing a European culture to the New World, which he said was only full of Indians and no culture at all. It became clear later, that he was not doing it for culture's sake, but doing it for improper reasons, and the Indians had plenty of culture of their own, thank you very much.

Here is why I so despise him: none in Hungary knew so at the time, but the Count was being paid money by the government of the Dominion of Canada for immigrants to come, Canada needing people to populate the western part of the Country, using cash to slow the flow to Pittsburgh, where so many Hungarians went. Yes, you may not believe, but the Count was on the Canadian Dominion Government payroll as a paid immigration agent not revealing the real reason of his interest, saying it was for culture and a desire to be helpful, but it was for the money, breaking up perfectly happy families, parents going away first, saying they would pick up their kids next year, some never picking up their kids ever.

Many families were broken up permanently by this, not being able to save enough cash in the new world to sail back across the Atlantic and then collect their children. Some families broken up this way remain so, even to this day.

So, now hearing all the facts on it, perhaps you too might agree that Count Paul Oscar Esterhazy was indeed a Judas, leading people astray, trading families for money, just a slave trader in finesse. On top of it, he wasn't a real Count! You might be surprised at that one! It came out later that the Esterhazy family in a Budapest newspaper accused Count Paul Oscar of being a phoney Count, a pretender, improperly using the Esterhazy name.

Not to be thrown from balance by such an accusation, arguing the matter in public the Count claimed that he was indeed of royal blood but fathered out of wedlock by the Crown Prince of Hungary. This was solemnly reported to him by his mother, he said, who was the other party involved, passing this information to him on the occasion of his twenty-first birthday, his coming of age. In this public statement, he said he had remained silent on such an important matter all these years out of a respectfulness to the Esterhazy name. But now challenged in public it was necessary for him to bring the chance fathering out.

My Oma later told me that the Count might be correct about this chance fathering since everyone knew that the Crown Prince, the alleged father, was often seen with ladies of the cabaret classes.

This would include the pale and comely Widow Boros, wife of the late Jonas Boros, the celebrated Hungarian novelist.

To which my Oma says with all humour intended, "Hmmmmm. The imperial prince of Hungary, has been sleeping in a dead man's bed."

And too bad for the alleged father, by the fact that there were very few birth controls available at that time except by retreat or by safes, and these safes were very poor products indeed, made from sheep intestine, the end tied with fisher thread and not very effective. This was properly proved in the Count's case, him being born in the first place. So, all evidence in, is the Count a Judas goat?

Yes, and yes again.

And by his own allowance, a bastard on top.

I WILL CALL THIS THE DAY OF LEAVING. AS YOU MIGHT suppose, there was not much in the way of entertainment in Becse and the very idea of one of the families leaving for the New World, for Esterhazy, Saskatchewan, thousands and thousands of miles away, was a big event. The train came by on Saturday and everyone in Becse showed up for it. It was like a carnivale this was, the horses wearing their best harness, all horsemen having two sets of harness, one for work and a fancier set for special events, this being a special event, the shiny, best harnesses were seen everywhere.

A little platform is built, the mayor standing on it and addressing everyone, talking about the adventure of those leaving for Canada, taking the opportunity to display his importance, him saying how he personally knew Count Esterhazy, ignoring the facts of the matter and telling everyone what a fine family this was, name-dropping in other words like any other politician, puffing himself up, a matter of self importance.

So, the whole town was treating it like a celebration, none thinking that I and my sisters and brother were about to become as orphans.

My mother and father, the centre of attraction now, barely paid attention to us with so much commotion on that day, all wanting to congratulate them on their departure and wishing them a great adventure, each being envious in a way, but each also being glad that they will remain here in Becse, where there are perfect certainties. And the few money lenders of the town were there too; every town having a few lenders and always present in case other citizens watching would be interested in this adventure to Esterhazy in Canada thousands of miles away and across an ocean. Emigrants would need to borrow money, and there were those who were willing to loan *forints*, in the belief that money would be easily obtained in the New World, and paid back in full and some extra, in the form of interest, showing a certain profit.

Just before my parents boarded the train, giving a public kiss to me, coming up close to my face, I could see in my mother's eyes the look of panic, in shock was she, not even knowing who we were, it seemed. Terrified, I think she was, at what was taking place, presenting a full break from her life in Becse, a trip across a scary ocean at the age of just twenty and nine, leaving her four children behind, a break from her mother, my Oma, leaving the place of her perfect childhood. Myself, I still don't know how I felt on the day my parents left Becse on that too long trip to North America. I might not have been upset. I can't remember now. On previous times, my mother and father would to go to the big city of Budapest, perhaps to attend to some legal matter or visit with old family members, occasionally just a tourist trip to see what's new. And this didn't feel much different. But this was surely greater than a trip to Budapest, the whole town in attendance, but it was quickly over in just about an hour. After the train left, my mother and father on it, we returned to Oma's house and suddenly everything became very silent. No one said anything in the house for almost a week. Usually, we were a very talkative household. But now, only Opa would move the pages of the calendar to speak once in a while as the days went by, saying such as, "Well, they must be in Budapest now." Four days later, "Well, they must be in Trieste now." And then, "Well, they must be boarding the ship now." "Well, they must be in the Mediterranean now." "Well, they must be on the Atlantic now." "Well, they must be in the middle of the Atlantic now." "Well they must be approaching Halifax harbour now" and on, and such, following their dangerous trip, his finger pressed heavy on the pages, a worried look on his face, if not openly admitted. He was aware that thousands of miles are now between him and his daughter, my mother, a love of his life. Not as it is now, there were no aeroplanes at that time, no quick travel. Opa had good reason to believe that he had seen his daughter for the last time.

And Oma grieved in a different way. She cooked. And for at least a month after their departure our everyday meals became as rich as only our Sunday meals once were. It was as though she was trying to make up to us for the loss of our parents, with rich foods. She made *borjuporkolt*, which is made from veal and she made *okorfarok ragu*, a kind of stew and my favourite, *paprikascsirke*; almost every day a meat dish. My fat sister Klara was in her glory. All she could talk about was the food. She, being older than me, went to school in the mornings, I went to school in the afternoons. Instead of saying hello to me to be polite, when our paths crossed, she going home, me going to school, she would not even say hello, just to ask what Oma made for lunch, hoping for something rich tasting. I got tired of this business. So one day, again our paths crossing to and from school, she saying, what did Oma make for lunch? Annoyed by the same question again and again and again, I said, "Oh something you will really like Klara.

It's really good. You will love it. Today she is making a special dish – shit with rice." Klara ran off screaming. She was offended, the idea of that being in her rice.

And she told Oma what I had said. When I returned home that evening, I was severely punished. I was made to kneel in the corner of my bedroom, and since rice was the subject of the offence, Oma put a handful of raw rice on the floor, on which I had to kneel. I brushed some aside, putting my knees down only on clear spots, but later Oma examined my knees and seeing no impressions, said I cheated on the punishment, made me kneel a half hour longer. And think, she said, think of what you did. Using foul language to your sister. I had to spend the evening in there, as a result.

To be truthful what happened in the weeks and months to follow, after my parents left, we kids started to misbehave. Maybe Oma and Opa felt sorry for us, and let us get away with too much, perhaps spoiling us. Maybe, we were angry at events as they were and had become rebellious. It was probably a whole bunch of things that made us go this way, but bad, we were. Just awful. Oma and Opa, now in their sixties, were given a handful; their own children grown and married and away in Canada, were raising still another family and probably too old and tired for the job. But there it is.

My sister Klara, I think was the nastiest of us. Oma would get up very early to do some work in the barn, feeling sorrow for Opa, helping Opa, him with one leg amputated. She never failed to leave breakfast for us on the table. Hungarian breakfasts are always a thin soup and a biscuit, very healthy. Awful Klara would grab my biscuit and rub it on an oozing sore that she always had on her upper arm, a sore that never went away, that almost kept her out of Canada when immigrating, later as you will hear. She rubbed my biscuit into that, so I wouldn't want the biscuit.

So, we became bad. Not bad, bad. But bad enough. Especially for Oma and Opa who had to control us. We stole fruit from the neighbour's orchard, which we would never have done before. Later Oma would need to apologize for us, making such excuses to the neighbours saying, "Well, they are only kids, and their parents are gone, and everyone should feel sorry for them."

An example: now, it is two months since The Leaving, and it is plum season. The plums are ripe. Surprise to us, the son of the neighbour from whom we had stolen fruit, said to us, "The plums are ripe on our trees, why don't you kids come over and get some." We were glad to. So, we are standing beneath the tree, the boy says, "I'll climb to the top and shake some off, the top is where the best ones are." He is up there in the tree and he is throwing some plums down saying, "Pick up the shiny ones, they got the most sun, they are the sweetest."

And indeed they were. The shiny ones really were sweet. But I have a very good nose and soon the shiny fruits did not smell of freshness to me. They smelt funny, to tell you the truth, but sisters Klara, Hanna and my brother were filling up on them. But I quickly look up, and I see the most appalling sight. The boy is picking the sweetest plums, from where the sun shone warmest, at the top of the tree, but he is sticking them into his knickers, into his pants, into his bare bum really, and tossing them down, saying the shiny ones thrown down were the sweetest, from where sun shone. But where he was putting them made them not to smell so fresh, and that's probably also how they got shiny, being moved around.

Boy is in the tree. We are on the ground. I told my sisters and brother of what I had seen the neighbour's boy doing. We shouted to him, saying we had enough fruit now, and we were going home. The boy came down, all laughing and jovial, laughing a little too much I think and proud of his achievement, until Klara, big fat Klara, jumped on him, held him down while I pulled his pants down and told my brother to fetch some hot Hungarian peppers from the nearby garden, the white Hungarian hots, hotter than the red hots, and bring them over and I rubbed those white hot peppers into the very place where he had earlier put the plums, punishing if not him, that offensive part of his body. I rubbed them over everything saying, dirty boy, dirty boy, dirty boy. And then we let him go screaming home. The mother complained to Oma, saying we were wicked, embarrassing a boy by pulling down his pants, his privacy exposed, to girls. Oma tried to tell the mother that the children were upset with their parents leaving and all, and she would not punish them this time, but if ever they did so again, please to let her know.

Kids being kids, in spite of the stinky plums and the hot peppers remedy, still we were friends with him that summer. Whenever we were in his garden, I would pick up a hot pepper and wave it slowly in the wind, and he would laugh and laugh, him picking up a plum and polishing it slowly, offering it to me, his arm outstretched a sneaky smile on his face. And we would laugh, and laugh, and laugh. For eighty years have I not seen him; I cannot even remember his name now, but if he is still alive, I hope he thinks back to that time, sometimes remembering what little devils we were at that time and what a good time we had.

He was a wonderful boy, regardless of those plums.

I WOULD WANT YOU TO GET TO KNOW MY FAMILY, SO NOW I will describe family members. First, there is Oma, the oldest, and she is the smartest being my opinion; born to the most politically influential family in Budapest, her father, a judge and highly respected, invited to every important occasion she said, his coat collar even finished in pieces of velvet, proving then, much as now, that persons are given good regard by the clothes they wear. The presence of those velvet collars indicating that this coat had been fashioned in Budapest and not the rural

Source: Family Archive.

Oma & Opa.

village of Becse, the wearer a substantial person, a person of importance presenting imported velvet collars of such soft beauty, symbolic to the upper classes.

So, when Oma came of marriageable age, naturally her parents believed she would wind up in the cultural city of Budapest, the wife of an influential, in other words a person equal to her status, she attending many velvet-bedecked social events. But that's not how it turned out. My Oma married my grandfather, an ordinary peasant. Nor was this a mistake as some might feel because the two got along so well, even though he was just a simple peasant carpenter, and she of privilege. A good choice she made I still think, because never in my growing up did I hear a cross word between these two. Oma and Opa were soul mates in a most romantic sense. Intended for each other, collected from the opposite ends of society.

But then of course, the tongue-waggers of the town were busy also, most to say, I would hear it often, that Oma was just a spoilt privileged person, a spoilt daughter of the judge, wilful, rebelling against parents, as some do even now, marrying beneath her station to spite her family, making her own choices, regardless. Not so. Oma had no spite against anyone, but what would you do, if you just happened across a perfect soul mate, taking joy in him, perfect but penniless. Think of it. What would you do? I think you would say Oma did the right thing.

And like anybody else they had problems to deal with, too. For example, Opa had only one leg mentioned earlier, the left leg run over by a threshing machine and amputated. After the amputation, being a carpenter and all, he made a wooden leg for himself; indeed he made two models. One was a false leg he used for farm work; it was a simple peg leg, like in pictures of pirates, made from a cedar tree bough, light and very effective. And amazing it was, to watch him follow the horse drawn plough, using his peg leg, capable even under these circumstances, his horse pulling, Opa keeping up no matter how quick the horse, us kids even giving applause to him at the row's end, encouraging him on, giggling and having a good time. Yes, he could do most things, even with only one good leg. He could even clean the chimney, up there on the roof to be seen, his peg leg put to purpose, straight out against a gable, holding his balance in the wind, going about his task with ease, the chimney needing to be cleaned in autumn, the storks using the chimney to nest a stork family, the nest removed at season's end. Well, the nesting of the storks was always welcomed no matter what the inconvenience, and considered a good omen, but the nests had to be taken out of there for the winter, dear friend, or we could not use the fireplace.

And then Opa had his Sunday false leg, which he also made. This was from oak, properly shaped as the real leg would have been, with a shoe on the end. It looked very life like and except for his limp, which he could concentrate away if necessary, if attending a formal event like the town's annual New Year's Eve Levee, to which my grandparents were always invited, Oma being who she was. And at these events, Opa never limped, him concentrating it away, even dancing, although in a somewhat awkward manner, if a Viennese waltz okay, but sitting out the Hungarian *czardas*, which is a very vigorous dance and requiring both legs in lengthy use. In the past, it was as a dance of the peasantry; sophisticated persons would not bother to do it, fearing to be demeaned. But, listen to this, when the Budapest composer Franz Liszt started using czardas rhythms in his famous Hungarian Rhapsodies, everybody started dancing to it; music earlier considered too rural suddenly becomes popular since Mr. Franz Liszt, the important Budapest composer, sees the value of it; everybody else following. But it is a fact, Opa enjoyed dancing the *czardas* very much until his left leg was cut off.

And then there was Opa's daughter, my mother, who I am sad to say, wasn't a smart one. I didn't think so as a child, nor do I think so now. A good enough lady, honest and sincere, but overly nervous, too often given to the vapours, taking to bed at every problem, ferreting herself away, avoiding decision making, waiting for all complications to pass. You would wonder how she could be the child of Oma and Opa, being so very different.

But my grandmother! My Oma! Oma! Oma! It was she who held my interest. She was always doing, or analyzing, or trying to understand even the smallest of events to the biggest. And there was no gossip in her, only trying to understand the facts, coming out with: Why did this happen? Why would that happen? Figuring things out, and putting it in a nutshell.

And I will speak of my siblings, Klara, Hanna and Bela. Dear fat Klara, the heavy eater in our family. I believe nervousness made her do it, trying to satisfy a frustration perhaps, even taking my morning biscuit as I said earlier. But also, she could be most generous in other ways if the humour took her, though never generous with food, food being a separate issue.

And my brother Bela, the middle born of the four of us, and Bela was just Opa all over again, a lookalike with the same behaviours. So much alike there were townsfolk who would say, in a jokey way, that Opa was the original, and Bela was sent from God as a spare, in case something went wrong with the original, this being said in a humorous way, nothing serious of course.

Then there is Hanna my other sister, good in school but not interested in much else; very conventional I would say, and she stayed that way all her life; she was a very predictable person. So, these are my list of siblings at the time, more added later under some unusual circumstances.

And now I will need to speak of the man my mother chose as her husband, eventualizing as my father. A most complicated man. A poet in his natural self, but a cobbler as his occupation, a maker of shoes really, but fussing over them, making them perfect, using leather from only the same animal, the same pelt, so they would match perfectly, giving the same grain and thickness, the two boots to be absolutely identical. The trouble is, when you treat shoe cobbling as art, it becomes unprofitable. None can pay the high cost of the cobbler examining each piece of leather carefully for thickness and grain, to make a perfect pair of boots, working slowly, cutting with certainty, taking plenty of time with the lasts.

And that's just how he ended up in Esterhazy, Saskatchewan. Authorities told him that the Northwest Mounted Police would need riding boots of this high quality. Flattering the poet-cobbler, my father, much work would be offered and any amount of time necessary to make the Mounties their boots would be available since the government is paying by tax money anyway.

My father bought the biscuit. To make boots at his leisure, cutting this, honing that, creating perfect riding boots, each a work of art. He was eager for the freedom of producing riding boots of the highest quality for the Northwest Mounted Police in Canada, and to be given plenty of time and materials to do so.

My father was a dreamer.

MONTHS GO BY AND I HAVE NOT HEARD FROM MY parents, no letter, or no word. Some of those returning from the New World reported disappointment with how things went there, returning to Becse now poorer than before, with a debt to be paid off in borrowed money taken in the first place, for passage. Those who returned came back with new debt.

But no word for me, from them, and I am imagining all kinds of bad things, such as the ship has sunk, my parents drowned, missing and never again seen. Opa tries to explain to me that it takes just as long for a letter to get to Becse from Esterhazy, Saskatchewan, as a person traveling would, in that huge land of Canada, the letter being posted in Esterhazy, thousands of miles away, needing to travel by rail to Toronto, Ontario, on to Halifax to be boarded on a ship to cross the Atlantic, he says, just like people, no different, through Trieste, and then by rail to Budapest, and on to Becse. "It takes a long time my little one," as they both called me, being so little for my age, at birth the size of a piglet, the runt of litter to boot.

So, there was no word from them. I would ask every day, or go to the postal station, asking Mr. Tinodi, where my letter would be. Mr. Tinodi was a teaser. He would pretend that there was indeed a letter here for me, but did it come yesterday? Did I not receive it yet? Maybe it has been misplaced, perhaps picked up by a person or persons unknown. Perhaps it is in someone else's file? I knew in my own mind that he was kidding about all this, he being basically a mean bastard, and it would bring my excitement up, making me to feel uncomfortable, him gaming me, probably bored with his occupation, although postal master was the best job in town, handed out for political involvement. And I would ask myself I remember, walking home, why people with good jobs would do things as such, teasing where it is unnecessary, making others uncomfortable. Oma never teased anyone ever, always being direct.

But Mr. Tinodi had problems of his own. The matter of his dead son of just twenty years, a braggart much like his father. Bad enough to lose a son, but worse to lose the son through stupidity. Here is what happened: the son, one evening over indulging with wine at the town's inn with some of his so-called friends, he was asked if he thought himself a brave person. "Of course," he says, "bravery runs in my family. My Uncle Ferenc served with the great statesman Lajos Kossuth, very much responsible for ending Hapsburg rule in Hungary. If it were not for my Uncle Ferenc, you idiots would be speaking Austrian, not the wonderful tongue of Hungarian. And under Austrian control you can bet that our paprika, our great national seasoning, would be substituted by caraway seeds. Caraway seeds in the goulash, can you imagine? And these wines," now he raises the glass to the candle, "these fine Hungarian wines coming from the Tokaj region, would not be the dry wines of our favour, but the sweet junks the Austrians drink. Can you imagine, such wines?"

Now in a cheeky way one townsman said, "Well, we are truly grateful to you and your dear uncle for doing all these important things; for being brave and all, and we know that bravery runs in your family, but we would like to test your bravery, just for the sport of it. Are you willing, here?"

"Of course," said the postmaster's son once again proving how stupid he could be, saying with much braggadocio, "A challenge from you is a command for me. I am indeed fearless, as was my uncle to whom you owe your state of grace."

Then, the chanting begins. The whole table chanting:

To the crypts alone
To the crypts alone
No dogs allowed
To the crypts alone...

Now the postmaster's son is beginning to feel concern; feeling a trick is up, but with no way to prove it. He says, "To the crypts?"

"Yes, we want you to go to the crypts on the hill in the cemetery, alone at the midnight hour, tonight. While you are at the crypts, we will honour your effort by drinking these fine wines from Tokaj region, which incidentally, we would not now be enjoying were it not for your Uncle Ferenc who served so well with Kossuth, ending the despised Hapsburg rule. Also, thanks to him for making possible the absence of the dreaded caraway seeds from this goulash, another plus due to his bravery, for which a great nation gives thanks."

Now, the speaker reaches to the back of the bar where a scabbard rests. It is a long scabbard, from which he draws an equally long broadsword. "Now," he says, "at midnight tonight, as a test of bravery, we want you to go to the cemetery, accompanied by neither man nor dog; go to the crypts on the hill, kneel to the ground, and speak a private prayer for us, in dedication to your Uncle Ferenc, to whom we owe so much. As proof that you have carried out this act of bravery, thrust this broadsword into the ground, leaving it there for our inspection at daybreak. This would be proof that you were there. In the meantime, we will remain here at the inn, drinking this fine wine, but you my friend will be executing an act of bravery. The crypts are extremely spooky and I doubt that any of us here drinking would have the courage to do as such, but of course for you, this is a small thing, indeed."

The stupid postmaster's son is in a bind. But he has been filling the room with his maleness and is therefore required to take up the challenge. At a quarter to midnight, fully wined, he picks up the broadsword, saying he would be back in a half hour, save the last glass for me.

Next morning he is found dead. He died, kneeling in the dark. Fulfilling his obligation, giving a prayer for Uncle Ferenc, he had thrust the broadsword into the ground, but in so doing, he somehow pushed it through his cloak, pinning himself to ground. Trying to get up in the pitch black of night to leave, broadsword through cloak, he feels being tugged. Now begins the panic. It feels as though the crypts are pulling at him, coming alive, angered at his impudent midnight visit!

Each time he tries to rise, he feels pulled to the ground. He can't get his breath. He actually dies of fright it is said, having swallowed his tongue. Choked himself to death over a foolish matter.

That was the end of the stupid postmaster's son #1.

Now there is son #2 being an interesting case in itself. Want to hear that one, too? The postmaster sacrificed much to educate son #2, who was a weak student at school but through much political manipulation the postmaster gets him a seat at the famous Eötvös Loránd University, in Budapest. This is a Jesuit institution and a very big deal, indeed. This is all the stupid postmaster talks about when you go to pick up your mail. "Oh yes indeed, my son is doing fine at Eötvös Loránd University," him mentioning the school's name at every opportunity as a point of pride. "He is much loved by his classmates and academically he is perfect."

The son actually graduates. Manipulation in high places, surely. To acknowledge this achievement, the postmaster gets the city council to plant an oak tree in the son's honour, trees being planted for noble purposes all the time in Becse.

City officials show up for the event. It is a nice day in July and the postmaster has collected all friends and family members and persons of importance to the planting of the oak. The son is very proudly there, too. Everybody around. The hole is dug with the town's silver shovel, and the oak placed in it. The dirt is returned to the hole and there is much applause. Now, the son carrying on much satisfied conversation with those in attendance, playing the part of a highly educated person, no longer from Becse is he, but from Budapest, for goodness sakes. Not a rural townsman is he now, but a cultured city person. He puts his one foot forward on the metal end of a garden rake, lying on the ground, tines upward, for raking around the newly planted oak and says, "and what instrument is this?" like he didn't know rural instruments.

So, as Oma tells it, when he pushes down on the metal end of the rake, tines upward, a matter of physics begins, and the long handle of the garden rake comes flying up at great speed, striking the postmaster's son on the forehead. Now the injured student falls to the ground, staring fully stunned. Big commotion. Everyone in the planting party becomes very concerned, gathering around the fallen student, applying wet cloths, two peasant women actually praying.

So, as Oma tells it, what was supposed to be a dignified event became despoiled. How the highly educated university graduate is knocked to ground, made senseless by a rural garden rake, the incident proving clearly that none should put on airs. This story was often repeated in our town whenever a case of vainglory showed up.

I WOULD NOT HAVE YOU BELIEVE THAT OPA WAS A LOSER where Oma's standard of living was concerned. She had a very nice house here in Becse, long and narrow rather than wide, which Opa built for us, him being a carpenter and able to do all the work on it his ownself. It was constructed slowly, not as today. This was built slowly and with consideration, the plans drawn on the kitchen table, Oma wanting this, Opa wanting that, even the kids offering suggestions, perhaps the kids making too many suggestions, Opa telling us to put a lid on it. Well, we were only trying to be of a help.

First built was the main room, a huge room, curtained at the corners to provide sleeping areas, bedrooms being added to the house as time and money would permit. Most of the wood for such gathered from the community forest, the logs taken to the sawmill and turned into boards, the boards returned to our plot, and slowly the house expanded to fit our needs. Most important was the fireplace constructed from ceiling to floor of river rock and field stone, fashioned with a huge oven in front. Even by today's standards a beautiful house. Many happy meals were cooked in that fireplace, but best of all was the caramel candy Oma would make from cane sugar when we could get it, dropped on the hot rocks, the sugar melting, and cooled with water, peeled off the rock and sucked by the kids. It was the finest caramel you can get. And bananas! Rarely were bananas available in Hungary at that time and even today, ask any Hungarian, and his favourite food would be the bananas. I still love them. When I was a child, I probably got one banana a year and that would be whenever they were available in the town's outdoor market. But that was it. Just one. You can bet I have eaten many bananas since, not being able to pass the supermarket fruit exhibit without picking up a pound or two.

In Becse, the town's outdoor market was very important to us. For the very little cash money our household needed, Oma would take a few pounds of butter, or eggs, or such, which she would sell for cash. I would always want to go with her, but forbidden was I, her saying I was so small I might become lost, or spirited away by gypsies she would threaten me, taken to their caravan as a new daughter, she would say, raised as a gypsy, away from your family, given in marriage to a gypsy, made to forever travel, never to settle down. She would say these things, laughing all the while, to keep me away from the market.

But she failed in this. Forbidden to market, I would pretend to be sleeping. Hearing her leave in the dark of the early morning and waiting a few minutes, I would sneak out of the house and cut across the road and then to follow the far side of the hedges, avoiding being seen by Oma, arriving at the market just minutes ahead of her, me jumping up and down, saying, "I am here, I am here." And always, she would pretend to be angry, saying that I was as quick as a spark off a fire, small and skinny, was I, but as quick as a spark off the fire. And she wondered why a little kid would want to do this, so early in the morning. To be truthful, I just always wanted to be with Oma.

The only time I was really angry with Oma was this: I was walking across the river bridge, looking down I saw a gunnysack floating. I thought this was wasteful, gunny sacks being expensive and rare, most made in Egypt. I thought I would fetch it with a stick for Opa. This I did, but upon opening the gunnysack, wet and shivering there was to be seen a tiny gray kitten, which unwanted, someone had taken to drown.

I took both home.

Opa was delighted with the free gunnysack. Oma was less pleased with the kitten, having several already, but I intended to keep it, mewing as it did, me giving it cow's milk, the kitten getting the shits from such an abrupt change in diet. But no matter, I cleaned its little bottom, named it Zsigmond, a noble's name, and in just one day it became an important thing in my life.

I put it to bed with me. Next morning when I awakened, it was gone. Oma said it had died and she buried it she said to save me the grief. But I did not believe her. It had been purring next to my ear when I fell asleep, saved from a terrible death it was, given a warm place to sleep, secure at last, he was happy. But my Oma lied to me, yes she did, to tell me Zsigmond had died; lied to me like a common person, disappointing me, like many other persons would disappoint, in years yet to come.

It surprised me that my Oma would do such a plain thing. Why? Why would she deny me to have Zsigmond when I was willing to look after him? We had other cats, sure, but this one was special, saved as he was from a watery grave by luck.

What did she do with him? She would not kill him, I am certain about that one, because like most villagers, Oma had a great respect for animals. Even the slaughter animals for meat were treated properly. We would always have a pig, which we fed on kitchen scraps and grain, but the pig was never slaughtered by we who raised it. Always a stranger would be asked to do it in. And we were forbidden to give the animal a name, just calling it "the pig" because giving it a name would give it a persona, making the necessary killing of it more difficult. The Good Book says: "Hit them and eat them." Well, the Good Book is a little vague on some of these matters when saying hit them, meaning to slaughter them.

Chickens too, were kept nameless. And whenever Opa needed to slaughter a chicken, he would take it, and before slitting its throat, he would take the knife and scrape the soil making a little grave for the blood, letting the blood flow into the ground, covering over, giving a kind of respect for the chicken, even if killing it.

The same consideration was given to pigs and sheep. All the animals were given special consideration, treated kindly even if being raised for slaughter. That's exactly how it was.

I guess you could say that in Becse, the slaughter animals were given many, many good days, and then just one bad one.

ANOTHER LETTER FROM CANADA. THIS TIME FROM Toronto, in the Canadian province of Ontario. Yes, they are both in good health. Yes, the weather is fine. Sure, they are making progress toward Esterhazy in Saskatchewan, but again more problems have cropped up. My parents were having difficulties in Toronto in trying to be understood when speaking, having a very limited knowledge of the English language. And also, the Canadian money is very confusing they said, with no relationship to Hungarian currency. The Canadian ones with a picture of King George of England on it, and although the numbers on the money are the same as on Hungarian money, the value of the numbers is quite different, making the use of Canadian money a difficult matter.

When paying for a meal for example, my father remarked that he would put all his cash on the table, trusting the waiter to remove the proper amount. For transportation, the same thing there, offering the entire amount held in his open hands, the driver invited to remove the correct tariff. Well, the proper amounts were not being removed with my father getting stoved every time, the supply of money quickly running out. Could more money be sent under these trying conditions? He went on to say that he would appreciate a quick reply in this matter, to the address of where they were staying in Toronto. And yes, they were staying with another Serbian family. This contact had been found by asking around the Toronto Union Train Station, "Are there any Serbian families around here?" One gentleman directing them to the Serbian section of Toronto. And yes! Again, they found lodging with Serbs, the only fault with this one my father said, was that the coffee served was the latté type, and not the boiled bean kind that Hungarians prefer, but other than that everything was fine. But this will be a short stay with the Toronto Serbs, my father wrote, and then on to Esterhazy, to the rewarding task of making riding boots for the Northwest Mounted Police. And in closing, in the P.S. of the letter, another reminder that the money part should be taken very seriously, "To please forward at the earliest opportunity."

Money problems, again. Whenever serious problems came to our household, Oma and Opa would switch to speaking

German, which they had a good knowledge of, to keep the kids from becoming too concerned, the kids knowing only Hungarian. Well I am sad to report, much German was spoken following this latest letter, it was just German, German, German, and not in a jokey manner either, always with a serious outlook.

So, this was again a request for money. And in amounts that Oma and Opa were not accustomed to, the amounts required for our household in Becse, so little. Requests here, for hundreds, unheard of amounts.

And what a silly situation if you can imagine, to have dinner, and then asking the waiter to pick up from all the money placed on the table, the correct amount. How naïve! How silly! *Learn* the values! Learn what the denominations *should* be when changed from forints to dollars. It's *elementary*! How much longer can you continue on your trip, giving responsibilities to others, doing nothing for yourselves, and then requesting additional money as need be? How much more will be required?

But, on the good side, they give you free Ogden's tobacco on the train, my father wrote, and free Coca Cola, too. Why? And what is Coca Cola? I didn't know at the time, but now thinking about it, both the tobacco and the Coca Cola were just free samples handed out by the manufacturer in the knowledge that immigrants not understanding English would learn the names of only *that* tobacco and only *that* refreshment, ordering only those at later times. This is just advertising and nothing special.

Well, my parents were still the centre of conversation in our town in Hungary. Word got around that my parents were now stranded in Toronto, and Oma and Opa were now refusing to send more money it was said. This was the talk of the market and the inn. Such terrible parents it was said, how they would not come to the rescue of their children. Sure, they had sold a cow to cover costs once before, but that was not a test of parenthood. Now, when real debt would rise, helping under those circumstances, now that is a true test.

That's how it is in little towns. Just yabble, yabble, yabble. Good to be living in one if you need help, bad when it comes to personal affairs, private information tending to leak out.

One morning, a knock at the door: "Good morning Mr. and Mrs. Aradi. How are you this fine morning? Can I come in please? No? Well can I talk to you on the porch, through the screened door then? I am Mr. Miklos the cattle drover who was here a few months ago, regarding the purchase of the cow. Did you finally get a good and proper price selling her locally, then? Good. It's always good when a cow is sold for the highest price and I am glad that this was as such. On other matters too, I am always willing to help, and I am wondering if you have another cow you might want to sell. You don't? Too bad since I am in the market for another creamer, and I hoped you might want to sell yours. You don't have another creamer to sell? Oh, too bad about that under the circumstances, because there is a very high demand for creamers at this time. An English Jersey would be especially nice. But I guess, if there is none to sell, there is none to sell, simple as that."

And his yabble yabble continued with: "But I have other ways of being helpful too; I am also available for cash loans to those who need one, if one is willing to sign a note against real estate. Not against livestock, which as you know from personal experience, can die. So the loan is against property, which is solid. And the money available can be in the thousands or maybe even in the hundreds of forints. The choice is yours. No? Not interested in a money loan at this time? And no livestock to sell for cash? No? So sorry. But if you ever need as such, just leave a note on the post office board, and I can be in touch. With a nice property like this one, there should be no problem. Nice lawn and flowers you have out here, too. And this is a beautifully built house. Just get in touch, if you want. Good day."

The cattle drover left and Oma did some murmuring, but in German of course.

"Did you kids tell him we needed money for Canada? You didn't? Who did, then? He comes here in a pesky manner, knowing that we have a money problem. I wouldn't borrow from him even for free, him taking advantage of folks in trouble. Out with him!"

Well, as you can expect with the circumstances being as they were, in the following days there was quiet in our household. Not pleasant. I made it a point to get out of the house as early as possible in the mornings, to go down to the river, to fish for crawlies, to fill in the time.

Later that same week Oma called me over to say that she would be going to Budapest to visit a cousin and would I like to go along, she saying she did not want to alone. "And being so skinny and small for your age, you can tell the train master that you are only five years old, so you will travel for free. I cannot afford two fares."

"But Oma that would be lying. You have always told us to tell the truth; to never lie."

"Well, my little one, no one likes to lie, but sometimes you need to. Sure, best to say the truth every time. Best to do that, of course. That's a certainty. But sometimes, like now when I don't have two fares, a harmless lie won't hurt." Now she smiles, and with a twinkling says, "My mother used to tell me, that the Good Lord gives every person a gift of twenty-five lies permitted without punishment, in a lifetime. And these are just white lies, not evil ones, just easy ones. At my age, I have very few lies left. But you, but you, you are only seven years; you probably still have most of them left. So? When we go to the train station on Wednesday, do the situation a favour, and spend one of those lies right then and there, because I don't want to go to Budapest alone, and I can't afford two fares."

"Would Opa go?"

"No. If Opa goes it will be two fares. If anyone else but you goes, it will be two fares. You can get on for free if you say you are five which you can do due to how small and skinny you are."

That's how it was with Oma. Always trying to make the best of it.

And so to the train master I said, "I am Zarah Petri, I go to Kisfaludy School, I am five years old and I am in the second year and I want to travel for free with my Oma."

Here I was, giving the train master more information than necessary, in nervousness.

"Five years old? In the second grade? Hmmmmm," said the train master, looking directly at me and giving a fish eye to Oma, "You must be a very smart little girl, to be in the second grade at the age of five."

"Yes, that might be true," I said, "they moved me quickly out of kindergarten because I am good with my sums." Whoops! Already two lies. Two gone from my lifetime supply. Two gone this morning already.

I didn't know what to further say. Nor did Oma.

Of course, the train master knew what we were up to, but he went along with it anyway. He gave us two tickets, the paid one, the yellow one, was Oma's. My ticket was light green, the free one.

Oma thanked him, saying God smiles down on generous deeds. All rewards are returned in the fullness of time. The benefits of every kindness is written in His Heavenly Book. Nothing lasts forever but kindness endures. He who helps the least of his brothers, helps himself, ya-ta-ta, ya-ta-ta, ya-ta-ta, etc., etc., etc. Thank you very much.

I WAS THRILLED. TO TRAVEL ON A TRAIN! FOR YEARS I had waved my arms at trainmen, as they sped by, the train with the smoke puffing out the top of the engine in a powerful manner, and they would always wail the whistle at me, saying in their own way, "Hi there. How are you? We are on our way to Budapest."

And now for certain, I was on the way to Budapest! Me and Oma. The two great travellers. Now breaking open our packed lunches that Oma had made for the trip; some fried bread with sour cream and greens, washed down with a shared bottle of cool lemonade. We were happy! This was the first time I had seen Oma giggle and laugh in some time with all the money worries coming in from Canada, and I wanted to feel responsible for her happiness this morning, even if knowing that perhaps it was just my free ticket doing it.

I remember everything about that trip. It may not be the same today, but the train coaches at the time, at least in my country of Hungary, placed the seats facing each other, the purpose to allow passengers, facing each other, to enjoy mutual conversations. Well, that's all well and good for adults, but children have a discomfort to that, not being able to avoid looking into the eyes of the stranger seated opposite. Staring. You can't *avoid* it. You are *drawn* to it, producing discomfort to both you and the stranger. I had quite a bit of that during the trip, my Oma engaging in conversation very comfortably with this passenger or that, but me being silently drawn to the eyes.

At one of the train stops, a man got on and moving into our booth, seated himself directly opposite Oma and me. Drawn to eyes as I was, this passenger's eyes were very strange indeed. To explain: the pupil of his left eye was not round as normal, but pear-shaped with the extra upper part extending into what should be the white part, the eye difficult for me to ignore with this arrangement. To say the least, it was most unusual. Indeed, I was unable to look in any other direction, drawn I was, to the sight of the pear-shaped pupil.

It became obvious to the new passenger, my interest in his eye, him finally saying, "I notice your little grandchild has taken an interest in my left eye."

Well, there was such great silence. And then me saying, "Oh, not at all. Not at all."

"No, no, no," said the passenger, "don't be embarrassed, I will explain. I was not born with this pear-shaped pupil," he said, his index finger stretched straight and pointing at it, "but received it about ten years ago, when not having train fare, the month of January. Bitterly cold it was when I jumped the train boxcar, riding on top. In the night in such cold conditions, the eye being just water really, the left eye frozen stiff. I knew it was froze when I got off the train. There was no pain at the time. But a head's ache was developing, along with a throbbing in the eye. I knew this was serious. How much worse could it get? I knew from experience that a frozen foot or a frozen hand, left unattended, rots. Can a frozen eye rot, too? Well, as you can believe, it was becoming apparent to me that I should not have stolen a ride on the train. I should have done the proper thing being as any train conductor would have allowed me on, as they usually do, if you tell them there is no money and you appear honest and trustworthy.

That's what I should have done, but that's not what I did. Pride made me steal a ride, instead of lowering my considerable pride and ask for a free ride, I was willing to steal a ride. But, once more I was lucky. As the morning moved along I needed to do something positive about my frozen eye, and so, putting my face to the sun, the sun's rays pelting down into the eye, lying there all morning, the good effects of the sun slowly revived it, and in a day or so, I regained complete sight, though the pupil remained pear-shaped as you can clearly see. I was told later that the eye had actually frozen, but the miracle of the sun occurred, the eye healing from sun effects and sight restored. I consider myself lucky, on this one. Sure, the eye looks a little strange now and all, an unusual eye but still a good one. Indeed, the sight from the misshapen eye is now stronger than the normal one. I think that this is much the same with people, sometimes the least among us, those we are about to discard, are the best of show. Mother nature does such things all the time. As you know almost every Hungarian village has an idiot. But is every village idiot *idiotic?* Think on that one. An example: our village idiot is never unhappy or displeased, but always smiling. And in this same town, we have the higher sheriff, an educated man, the smartest among us but he is the least happy. He is so unhappy that a fortnight ago he blew a cartridge into his head, killing himself instantly. So, as it shakes out, the smartest among us did an idiotic thing and the village's idiot is still alive, still asking direct questions, not beating about the bush, always seeking retorts. And that's why I chose to answer your granddaughter's interest about my eye. She will be richer for having met me today, to hear the explanation of the frozen eye, she is now better informed."

And on, and on. Ya-ta-ta, ya-ta-ta, ya-ta-ta! This passenger would not stop. The misshapen eye was a badge. Again, with the eye he went, on and on. He did several more reviews on his eye, the attitudes of others toward it, how it is often the centre of attention, how this affliction has actually proved to be an advantage, like now with the pear-shaped eye central to so many social conversations with others, and on and on, etc., etc., etc. And then finally, *finally!* thanks be given to God, a Holy Intervention I am sure, his point of departure arrives, the train stopping, now he leaves, tipping his hat, bidding good day.

When he left, Oma and I began to laugh. She did not say anything, nor did she permit me to say smarty things about the eye man, just to keep her hand to her mouth, trying to stare out the window, trying to distract herself for goodness sakes, trying to shut down her laughter, while I pulled my knees up to my chest, squeezing myself into the corner, losing so much control. But managing to keep the laughter down, if only to be polite.

That's how it went. But still, over all, meeting people on trains is such a good experience. Surely, I love everyone in my town, those I meet every day, having a history with each one, but I know them almost too well. Here on the train, with every stop, another person gets on, speaks for the first time, and I again meet someone new.

Now, a lady places herself opposite Oma and me. She introduces herself, her name I can't now remember, but she too, is going all the way to Budapest. And the purpose she makes clear. "I am going to Budapest to collect the body of my dead husband." This really fascinated me. Her dead husband. How? Why? When? Where?

"He was a good man, he drowned."

Good. She is going to begin with "how."

"He worked on the boats on the river Danube, at the ports in Budapest where he lies now. He got the idea to work on the boats about two years ago. The plot of land we were using for support, we were just renting, and the land was taken back by the owner, putting our family of seven out of any kind of support. So, he had to do something so he left for the boats and has been forwarding money to us to keep us going for those two years. But, as you can see, it has not worked out well, being now drowned."

Oma gave the woman a look of compassion, and the woman opposite, accepted such with grace, moving her head up and down, silence all around now, save the clicking of her dentures. And then, staring forward, "So, he fell overboard, and so Andras, that is his name, was never a good swimmer. You see, in the town he grew up in there is no river and without a river there is no training. So, he could not swim as much as he loved his job, yes, on the boats, sailing up and down the Danube going all the way through central

Europe on the boat, all the way to the Black Sea. He would come home to our humble village about twice a year, and would tell great tales of his travels, speaking intelligently about the kind of merchandise shipped, the size of the vessels that he sailed on. It was an interesting life, I allow, but dangerous, especially for a non swimmer like Andras. And now, I will need to pick him up. Take him home for the last time."

"I don't mean to pry," said Oma by this time becoming as curious about the woman's sad dilemma as me, "but how will you support you and your family with Andras, your husband, gone." This was a good question.

See? Can you see how my Oma would extend friendliness to everyone, now speaking of the woman's dead husband on a first name basis? Calling him Andros, by his Christian name? As though he was still alive? Being familiar? Expressing concern? This was typical of my Oma. And then she said to the widow, taking a wise phrase from the Irish saying, "Well, the men must work, and the women must weep."

And that is so true.

"Yes," said the woman, "that is so true. And now, the additional expense of bringing him home again, my fare going up there to collect him, and his coming back with me, I am becoming very short. Very short of money. And I am not to beg. As you know, we have no beggars in Hungary. Hungarians do not beg, it is not honourable. But I am afraid I am going to need to break with that, and when I get to Budapest, I will need to do so, going to the market area. Do you know where that is? What part of the city? I will need to go there and bring myself to beg in order to collect the body of my dear husband. Begging is shameful of course and should not be done and a good Hungarian will not do as such, but for me, I can see no other outcome."

So then Oma said, "Poor Andros, when did this awful accident take place?"

"Several days ago," said the woman, "I still grieve the event."

Now, interesting, after a brief silence Oma changed the subject, looking out the window, remarking that Budapest was now so different than when she lived there as a little girl, with so many Viennese living there now, she said that it is sometimes a surprise to even hear Hungarian spoken, Austrian being the most used language, now. And how the desserts served at the restaurants come mostly as Viennese pastries, rather than the much loved Hungarian *szilvasgomboc*, those wonderful sweet dumplings, stuffed with prunes, one time the regular concluder of Budapest meals, now no longer, just these sweet pastries being served today. "*Szilvasgomboc* is still my favourite," said Oma, "and I am certain they are no longer obtainable."

"Andros would have been forty-seven on his next birthday," said the woman.

"I hesitate to say so in front of the child," meaning me, said Oma, "but I am beginning to believe that war will come even to my town of Becse. There is so much civil unrest right now."

Now the widow lady was staring down to the area of her lap, a rosary present, she was slowly fingering the decades. Oma has always been reluctant to talk of her own problems, but I suppose because she could offer nothing to the widow lady she said, "Well, money is becoming a greater necessity than before. I can remember times after my husband and I were married, that money was never needed; we have our own little farm, and there is plenty of help from neighbours when it comes to getting the work done, but everything is changing so much now, with money becoming a most important thing."

The widow lady had a look of discouragement. With Oma mentioning that perhaps she had serious money problems too, now with my parents in Canada always needing, the newly widowed seemed to lose interest in our little group. She stopped fingering the decades on the rosary warming on her lap, and announced that her grief was now coming to a head, and so great that she would need to find a seat by herself, not wanting she said, to depress others.

And then she moved off, Oma nodding sadly in her direction.

Later we saw her seated, this time with several male passengers and presenting the same sorry look, a sadness evident, the rosary warming in her hands, expressing her shortage of money for the retrieval of her dear dead husband, and surely receiving money awards from these sentimental gentlemen, things working out okay.

WE WERE APPROACHING BUDAPEST, AND OMA appeared to be a little nervous. But I was excited. All my life, although only seven, I had heard of Budapest and persons speaking of it and its wonders. To be clear, Budapest is not one city it is two cities, Buda and Pest. They just say "Budapest" as though it were one. Buda is on the east side where the Royal Palace stands, and Pest on the west side, where the city zoo and park is.

The train chugged to a very slow stop, as though its mighty engine was tired from the pull all the way from Becse, and seeking a deserved rest after all the effort. We met at the station, by Oma's two sisters and their husbands, who were earlier notified by post that we were coming. That's when some disappointment began. Suddenly, Oma, who I always thought to be noble and beautiful, queensome really, suddenly took to looking plain to me. This was owing to the finery worn by her awaiting sisters, all bedecked in comparison, their hands in white gloves even though the weather warm, and a parasol each; their husbands holding such above the ladies' heads, even though a cloudy day. And may God forgive me for being unkind, Oma, wearing her best dress with which she took such pains to iron at home before leaving on the trip, now looking so plain, a dress of a single colour, no embroidery, and not to the floor as her sisters, but to calf length, the length for field work.

Nor did the kissing and shaking of hands help matters much. The gloved hands of the sisters, and Oma's hands, dark lines of work apparent on her hands, yes, and the faces of her sisters, milk white, and Oma's face deeply darkened by the sun.

These were noticeably different members of our family, accustomed to living in easy circumstances, as I am sure once Oma did. I remember whenever Oma mentioned her childhood she would always use the words, "in my earlier life," meaning her life before marrying Opa, him the peasant carpenter and cabinet maker. Well, today, her earlier life was becoming clear to even my child's eyes, this earlier life so different, so *fussy*.

And we were transported to the family home, not by horse and carriage, but by automobile for goodness sakes, the husbands sitting up front, busily engaged in operating the machine, pushing the "spark lever" up or down as required, the ladies not knowing what the "spark" was, the men indicating that a spark was required in igniting fumes cylindrically, and the "spark" would explode tiny beads of petrol, forcing down the cylinder, and making the wheels to move. This would be year 1917 and automobiles not common.

But I noticed that although it was fine to have an automobile transport us and not horses, the inconvenience of needing to shout at each other due to engine noise, was although tolerable, not pleasant. Nor was this much different than when using our horse and shay in Becse, the horse pulling heavily and occasionally giving a fart under pulling pressure, always making us kids to giggle and the grandparents giving a smile. The horse, pulling? Well, was the automobile engine not pulling too? Pulling hard? Making a similar percussive sound? Doing the same? Giving release? I believe this is a likely comparison.

We arrived at their house and I will describe it. This had an upstairs and downstairs, unlike our home in Becse, all on one floor. Stairs leading to the front door were constructed with separate steps on both sides, left and right. Later it was explained, that this was designed for modesty's sake, the gentlemen using the left side for going up, and the ladies the right side, no man following her as she needed to lift her long skirt, going up the stairs. This seemed pretty silly to me, but people living in Budapest have many, many rules.

Much fuss was made of our visit, with first being shown to our bedrooms, and although I would rather have slept with Oma, we were assigned rooms of our own. I started to feel homesick. I had been away only a day, but already too much had happened, and I would have given anything to be back in Becse.

Next day, a person of my own age was introduced to me, and she had been instructed to play with me, to fill the time. I learned that she was actually part of the hired household, her mother, the cook, and the young daughter employed as chambermaid. Her job was to keep the master bedroom neat and clean, fulfilling all requirements, tossing out the urine bucket each morning. That's what chambermaids actually did. I thought it was an embarrassing task; no child should be required to toss out urine buckets, filled by adults as a convenience.

Little did I realize that I would find myself in similar circumstances a few years later in Canada following the death of my father. I very much enjoyed the company of the chambermaid. She was from Baja, a small town, even smaller than Becse, and her mother came up to Budapest for domestic work and she had been here for almost a year. She said it was different from Baja, with many activities for adults but nothing much for children, although she had been to the Budapest Zoo and that was quite interesting.

I told her about my mother and father leaving for Canada, how my father would soon be building riding boots for the Northwest

Mounted Police, about the boy with plums in his bum, how Opa only had one leg; one leg amputated, held down by two men while the veterinarian removed it. I told her everything I knew, and she did the same.

Our evening meals were taken at a long table in a dining room, a room as big as our complete house at home, and after a few days Oma saying, "But I must be leaving," the sisters bidding her "Not to go," Oma coming out with "But of course I must," and the sisters, "Please don't, not yet," and Oma saying "But really I need to," and the sisters, "Why not stay another few days," and Oma, "No I really can't."

That's how it went.

As it turned out, next day the goodbyes were said, and we were taken by automobile to the train station, Oma's ticket already purchased, me traveling for free, due to my small size. As the train moved out, there was much waving from the platform, the sisters again in finery, the husbands holding the parasols above the ladies' heads, now making a little more sense this time than last, because at least this time the sun was shining.

For most of the ride home, Oma was silent. There was no fun. Finally, I asked Oma what the undisclosed matter was. She said, after a long pause, "Do not mention this to anyone at home. Not to Bela or Klara or Hanna and certainly not to Opa. I have come to my sisters and asked for money, to be sent to your parents in Canada. My sisters have willingly given such, and offered even more if necessary, and for this I am indeed thankful, having no other way out."

I thought about this for a few minutes and then using my good business sense, I said, "with no extra?" Meaning no interest added on top?

"No extra, no interest" said Oma. "No payment back, even. It was a complete gift."

A long silence and then I said, "If they gave gladly, then why Oma, are we so sad on this trip back?"

"My sisters have received all the payment required, and in full," she said now tearful, "since now they have proven themselves correct. Many years ago I left Budapest to marry and live in Becse with your Opa, the family was opposing this, saying I would spend my lifetime in need. This is exactly as it turns out. Exactly! My sisters are satisfied with the result. They have been proved correct, my little one, and they are pleased by it, shown in a patroness way. And so, in this particular matter, not in money or interest, but still I would say they have been well paid. The money means naught to them."

Returning to Becse, I said nothing to Klara or Hanna or Bela or to Opa about this matter. I said nothing to no one, being certain that Oma had been greatly humbled by this event.

"OMA! OMA! THE WAR IS COMING, THE WAR IS COMING!" I was running as fast as I could from the post office where a huge sign was placed by Postmaster Tinodi, instructing what to do when the war starts.

"What war?" said Oma, "What war are you speaking of? Is it the Serbs? There is war everywhere? War doesn't come to unimportant places like Becse. There is nothing here for them."

Well, as smart as Oma was, she was wrong about this one. This was the beginning of the First Worldwide War. War number one. The worst one, ever. None as bad, since.

So I said, breathless now from the running, "Postmaster Tinodi is giving instructions about what to do. He is also telling everyone that military officials are coming tomorrow, and to show loyalty we must tonight burn a candle at the front window, so loyalty can be counted by the officials."

Oma gave little notice. She continued with the making of *palacsintak* for supper, paying little attention to what I said, saying to reply, "But my little one, we will be wasting a good candle for foolish political purposes. Candles cost."

"Oma, Mr. Tinodi says that those who don't burn the candle are certainly going to have their windows smashed by patriots."

"Okay." said Oma, giggling, "If such is the case, we will burn the candle, my little one. Candles are cheaper than windows."

Can you hear that? Oma even coming up with humour under such dark circumstances. That's how it always was with Oma. Wit was always present. She always had something to say.

Now she was expanding things. "Maybe, we will even burn a candle in all the windows," said Oma, building the humour, "Maybe the side windows too. Maybe even a bonfire in the back yard."

Now, I was sure she was joking.

But dusk came. Slowly, looking out to the street, you could see candles beginning to show up in every house, more for the defence of the windows than for patriotism. Oma did the same. I guess she was thinking about those windows.

Next day, nice and sunny, a platoon of soldiers headed by a commander are standing around the post office talking to Mr. Tinodi. He is nodding his head in agreement. Mr. Tinodi is always nodding in agreement if talking with an official or the mayor or any person of importance, but scowling at ordinary citizens. Oma correctly said that Mr. Tinodi was a braun noser. I wasn't sure at that time of just what a braun noser is. As an adult now, I am quite sure.

Braun indeed was his nose, and very obvious. So later, I went to the post office hoping for a letter from Canada. Even the soldiers were quite nice to me, standing in front of the post office, one soldier even putting me up on his shoulders and walking around, saying that he had a little girl, much as me, at home, and he was now away for two years. And I felt proud, at least for a few minutes to substitute for his little girl, up on his shoulders, me, even at that early age knowing how he must have felt, how lonely, and I was glad to substitute.

But Mr. Tinodi, was being very official. He was saying to the Commander of the platoon, that yes, Mr. Aradi (my grandfather) has four horses, two more than necessary for his small acreage, and perhaps the Commander might be interested in taking two of those horses, for war usage.

When I heard this, I ran home as fast as possible, saying to Opa, "They are coming for your horses Opa, the army wants your horses."

Opa took me very seriously, unlike Oma and the candles. And indeed, they did come. Mr. Tinodi leading the Commander, talking in low tones, being very confidential. And then, Mr. Tinodi has the nerve to introduce the Commander to my Opa, like this is going to be a very pleasant visit. He says, "Mr. Aradi, the good Commander here needs your horses for the war effort. As you know, we are in battle now, as patriots, against a bitter enemy, and horses are needed very much in this struggle, and I have told the Commander that you have four horses, most people in the village, only two, and you would be glad to give two horses to the war effort."

Opa said he would not like to do this.

That's when things got bitter.

Opa said, "Yes I have four horses, but two of them are mares and are used for breeding purposes, providing cash income for the family.

"Let me see the horses," said the Commander, walking toward the barn, Mr. Tinodi hurrying to lead the way, still talking to the Commander in extremely friendly tones, proud to have given all this information about Opa's horses, doing so for future rewards.

Once inside, the Commander said he would take the two mares. Opa resisted, saying "I need all four horses but if you must, take the two geldings. The mares I would need for more breeding purposes which is most of my income; I sell at least two colts a year."

The Commander is starting to get awful. He orders two of his soldiers to remove the mares from the stalls. My Opa resists them, grabbing one of the men by the sleeve.

And now, I saw this. Things a child should never see. The Commander, powerful in this sharply pressed uniform, my Opa an old man with just one leg, and the Commander starts to beat Opa on the head using his riding crop. Mr. Tinodi turns his back to the action pretending he has nothing to do with this outcome. My Opa is being beaten like a school boy, just standing there, his hands covering his head, and the riding crop coming down on him, whomp! Whomp! Whomp! I am watching from the window. But strange, I am not terrified. I feel like this is not happening. It cannot be happening. They are taking Opa's mares. They are beating him on the head. He is standing, his hands above his head while the Commander whips him with the riding crop. Whomp! And next I see, the mares are taken away.

Opa did not come back into the house all that afternoon. He stayed in the barn. I don't know what he did in there. But he must have felt awful. He must have felt defenceless and no longer in control of matters. And when you cannot defend yourself, how can you defend your family, your children, in this instance, your grandchildren, their parents away, chasing an impossible dream to Esterhazy, Saskatchewan, to make riding boots of special leathers for the Northwest Mounted Police.

Impossible situations.

That evening, things got worse. Perhaps not to kill but to scare the villagers into behaving properly, the soldiers started shooting into every house, candle burning or not; every house got shot at. Our family scrambled under the beds, Oma telling us to keep our heads down, stay quiet, her body shaking, I could feel it.

Not even to this day can I forgive the military for creating such indignity, making my Oma and Opa now in their sixty of years, needing to cower beneath beds like fools. For me, this is unforgettable, unforgivable. My Oma, she who I had never before seen fearful, now under the beds hugging the grandchildren, me, Bela, Hanna and Klara, while the cowardly soldiers shoot bullets into all the houses of Becse.

They should be ashamed of themselves, even all these years later.

NOW, IT IS TWO YEARS AFTER THE CANDLE AND the bullets.

We have not heard from my mother and father, whether they arrived in Esterhazy, Saskatchewan, in Canada, safely, the war making the postal service unreliable. And by this time, sad to say, I am starting to forget about them. When they left me, I was seven. Now I am nine years. To tell you the truth, my Oma has become both mother and grandmother to me in the absence of my parents.

You cannot leave your children behind and expect things to be as they were. Would my parents expect they would be remembered by their children, just as they were? Did they expect no change as the children grew older? What foolishness to leave children behind in the care of other family members, the love transferred, perhaps gone forever.

My parents paid too much attention to Count Paul Oscar Esterhazy and his type, my poetic father wanting to make riding boots, in an artistic way, in Canada thousands of miles away, over the Atlantic Ocean.

And the First World's War has finally come even to Becse, with the candles and the bullets and the unlawful taking of horses. The war was begun first between Hungary and Serbia in 1914, lasting through to 1918, everyone getting involved, including thirty-two countries, important countries like Russia, and

England, and the United States. From just a little war, a big war grew. That is one reason why we were not hearing from my parents. Only government business was being conducted, the ships needed for the war effort.

And then, later, in 1918, at war's end, Hungary is carved up. The Banat region, where my beautiful town of Becse is located, is cut in half, with Serbia receiving the western part, now being part of Vojvodina, and Romania getting the eastern part, which is now part of Transylvania. What I am trying to tell is that my precious Becse is no longer a town in Hungary. After hundreds of years of being Hungarian, it is awarded to Yugoslavia, given to Serbia, to be exact.

That's what happens in wars, the carving up of the spoils, by the victors.

Schoolyard bullies.

O OMA CALLED US IN FOR A TRUTH CONCERT. What might a Truth Concert be? I will make it clear as I possibly can.

These Truth Concerts were popular with Oma. Whenever a family crisis came up, a farm animal gone ill, a financial problem arising, our behaviours perhaps at school, she would always call us in for what she called a Truth Concert.

Today she called for one, coming out especially important in nature, when she actually gave a time. "Everybody be here at two o'clock this afternoon. Everybody."

This was the first time she gave a time, this one being really special.

My siblings and I spent the morning wondering what this latest Truth Concert was going to be about. "Klara," I said, "Did you steal any fruit lately?"

"No, not since the last time."

This is the kind of foolish answer that you can expect at any time from my sister Klara. "Yours is not a proper answer, Klara. I am just wondering what this is all about. Oma and Opa have been very silent these past two days, showing something is wrong. To get her talking, I even asked Oma about life in Budapest, to get her started, but to no effect. So, there is something up."

We tried to think of what we might have done to bring on another Truth Concert, even Bela trying to remember some possible misbehaviours of his own, coming up empty handed, Bela rarely misbehaving.

We spent the morning at the river, flinging rocks, the flat ones especially, could be skimmed across the surface; we did it as a contest, the winner awarded a wish to be granted by the beautiful river naiad, Lady Iona. I can't now remember who won the wish.

We went home for lunch. Still no response from Oma and Opa, me asking "What has gone wrong, Oma?" and her saying, "You will find out soon enough. After we eat."

I should have suspected. This was not an ordinary lunch of potato pancakes or a dumpling dish, such as would be the usual, but a special meal, beginning with a ragout soup, seared chicken breasts, cucumber salad. Klara was really impressed. But I had learned from experience: special meals always meant something was up.

We have now eaten, if in silence. Still not two o'clock the appointed time.

Two came. We all sat down again at the table, Klara, Bela, Hanna, Oma and Opa, and me. And then Oma began the much-awaited Truth Concert, or tried to begin, because she had trouble getting it started.

She was losing control of conditions. As a little girl, I rarely saw Oma cry, she being a straightforward person, not given to putting on shows. But now she was crying deeply. Not out loud, but the crying was deep down, the sound muffled, her face on her chest, red from pressure. This was immense sadness. Opa too, was of the same mind, not making noise at all, but the tears were evident, flowing down his cheek, which he brushed away with his hand, collecting the tears on his palm, Oma using her apron for a similar purpose.

What had we done? Now, I started to cry, too, not knowing the reason, but the atmosphere by now was so sad, that this could not be avoided. Not knowing the reason for all this sadness had no effect. Just the atmosphere, the complete unhappiness showing up in the two people I loved most in the world, had this terrible result for me.

Finally, Oma took control. Just like that. Like the snap of the fingers, the tears were stopped. She said, "In the next month or so, or maybe just in weeks, your mother and father are coming from Canada to get you, to take you with them, away from Hungary to Esterhazy, in the province of Saskatchewan, in Canada. I received the letter on Tuesday. That's what was in it." We each were shocked. We each knew what this meant. I am sure, as much as Oma and Opa loved us, the work of raising us, the parents absent, was hard, and the responsibility too great, the uncertainty of our future a heavy burden. I did not believe then nor do I believe now that grandparents should be required to raise the children of their children. One family per set is well enough. So Oma and Opa should be relieved at my mother and father coming for us, ridding the burden, but made very unhappy by this too.

The bonding among the six of us was now much too strong.

And I wondered, how was it that Oma received the letter without me bringing it to her since I went every day to the post office.

That bastard postmaster, Mr. Tinodi! I had stopped in at the post office, sometimes twice a day hoping for a letter from my parents. I had done this every day, for more than two years. Now, getting a letter from Canada, Postmaster Tinodi knowing the importance of such, had personally hand delivered the letter to Oma himself, just to be part of an important event. Prouding himself. Being Mr. Bigshot. Having the ups.

Well, I put Mr. Tinodi on the same line as Count Esterhazy. Unkind hearts.

THE LONG ABSENCE OF MY MOTHER AND FATHER TOO greatly changed things in me. I knew coming back now they would remove me from Oma and Opa. To make events even sadder, on the day of my parents return, the town's arrival festivities were not nearly as large as the going away party. Only a few citizens showed up at the railway station, not even politicians making an appearance, emigrating families by this time being old stuff. Even Mr. Tinodi, the postmaster, not showing up, he who usually missed nothing, always making himself available for public events, a chance to present himself as a city official, improving his importance. Well, not even did he show up, proving just how common these events had become. Mr. Tinodi could be considered the last straw.

The train powered to a stop. And then started up again. Then it stopped again. Then it backed up a bit. Meanwhile, the passengers were leaning out the windows, first glimpse of my mother, she yelling at us frantically, feelings elevated, while the train jockeyed for unloading position, the passengers beginning to wonder if the train would allow them to get off with all this constant movement.

It finally did so. My mother coming off the passenger car now looked much different to me, her clothes unrecognizable, colourful now rather than the strong dark colours she wore while living in Becse. And she looked much older. When she left over two years ago she was small and fragile, now appearing in a much stronger form.

And she was obviously pregnant.

As a ten year old, even if a child, I was able to recognize the condition having seen it so often in the animals of the pasture.

In these matters I was sophisticated, full of information and able to identify and clearly determine. I didn't have the need of being told. And I thought further: had my mother actually travelled across the water from Canada to Trieste, and then by rail to Budapest, and south then, to Becse all these thousands of miles in pregnancy? Away from medical attention, away from simple comforts? How awful. Even the animals of the field I knew sought the comfort of a cool ravine in such a condition, away from hooplah. Pity for my mother tossed up and down on the Atlantic in a state of late pregnancy.

And so after the normal hugs and kisses of reunion, the adults quickly gathered to one side of the station platform to discuss adult matters, certainly the pregnancy being a surprise to everyone. I stood to the sidelines with Klara, Bela and Hanna, my siblings and waited in silence. I had knotted my handkerchief in the excitement and was now attempting to loosen it having little success with my best handkerchief the one with the blue anchors and the red polka dots, knotted beyond unravelling. I still clearly remember that part.

The wagon trip from the train station to Oma's house was a rather loud affair, everyone talking at once, my father eager to talk about his adventure. Oh, sure Canada is a great place. Oh, sure the Mounted Police enjoyed the boots he created for them. Oh, sure the winters are cold in Saskatchewan and Alberta. And yes of course, Esterhazy in Saskatchewan, is a beautiful place. Most of these positive words became discounted in the next few days as the real truth of the matter dripped out. His employment with the Northwest Mounted Police was very short lasting only about three months, the leathers being used he said were not appropriate. And then by chance, he found work farther west in the forests near Wetaskiwin, in Alberta, gaining employment there as a lumberjack, given a Swede saw to cut the wood by hand, paid by the cord, bonuses awarded for anything over seventy cords. He worked very hard, getting many cords. And then, my parents became especially lucky in the employment department, my mother receiving employment in the camp cookery, so doubling their income. Her Hungarian dishes won immediate approval, the camp managers even making an extra attempt to obtain the proper spices, including true Hungarian Paprika, not the smoked Spanish stuff, the Hungarian paprika made scarce by the war. "When are you going to make Beef Galoshes again?" the lumberjacks would say, my mother correcting them, saying not galoshes, that's winter overshoes, but *gulyash*, is the correct way, but they never got it straight. Even the Indian lumbermen went for that *gulyash*, paprika not a known spice to them, which they considered exotic.

So, with my mother working too, and nowhere to spend it, living as they were in the lumber camp, away from civilization, the money piled up quite quickly. This was a good thing too, because Oma had told me that the last money sent to Canada, would be the last sent ever, enough of this!

Financially, they were doing very well. Well, isn't that what everybody wants?

And now, making their stake in the Alberta lumber camp, they returned to Ontario, announcing they bought a farm, not like the piddly twenty-acre farms of Becse, but fully one hundred acres. One hundred! And these acres are in the most productive part of Ontario, the sandy loams of Simcoe, Ontario, he would tell us. And yes, sure, of course, there is a house on it. And a barn? Of course. Yes, and there is a town nearby with all the necessities available for purchase.

During the day I joined in the excitement about the farm in Simcoe, it was so big and valuable. But going to bed at night I would shiver at the prospect. The dark of the room, and the quiet of the night, made circumstances appear frightening. The idea of leaving this that I loved, for something uncertain, made me ill, elevating my fears, making me sick to the stomach. I would become filled with sadness. And I would say to myself in such grief, "Am I dying? Who is killing me? What can be done about it?" I had to talk to myself, self assess myself, hold my own Truth Concert, only me in attendance. "Am I dying? Who is killing me? What can I do about it? Is there any way out? Can I resist being taken away from here? Can I fight? If I fight, who will help me? Would my brother and sister help? Who else? Would there be help from anyone? Would Oma fight to keep me? I know she would want to do so, but could she dare challenge the wishes of my parents?" In those moments I felt like I was the property of others, not belonging to myself, yes and this is a feeling I would come to know many times in my adult life, this being only the first time, showing up again, and again; the lonesome feeling of not belonging to yourself.

If I died, I thought, it would be death by heartbreak. Can you die of this? I believe you can. And I wanted to die. And I imagined my death here, the adults finding my cold body in the morning, killed by events they put upon me, and they would feel sorrow, yes, sorrow and shame for taking me away from Becse, from Oma, from Opa, and my swims in the river Tisza, and my surprise trips to the market, me jumping up and down, saying Oma I am here! I am here! And she saying I am like a spark off the fire. What would the future hold for me, on a farm in Simcoe, an unnecessary place I had never been to, and place for which I have no feelings?

On August 21, 1921, my father, the poet, slapped me across the face. Hard. And for having a keen tongue. I remember the day well, the exact date, the slap occurring on my eleventh birthday, quite a birthday gift, and given because I had announced in a bold voice, that I would not be going to Canada with them, that I would remain here in Becse, that they should go, enjoy themselves, have a good time; I would remain here in Becse, this will always be *my* place.

And I shed no tears from the slap. I stood staring at the ground, waiting for a possible second blow that never came. I believe events were more than my father could handle. The poet in him could never take much pressure. Here is where I left the yard and went to the river.

At the breakfast table the next morning I said, okay, I would be willing to go to Simcoe in Ontario, in Canada, and the new farm but only if Oma and Opa went, too.

All, including my father laughed. But it was not a hearty laugh, a laugh of enjoyment. It was a laugh of criticism. Like, how foolish, how foolish of this little girl to come up with such childish suggestions. Oma and Opa laughed too, but understandably since I had not told them about the slap and they thought I was just fooling about this, coming up with humour perhaps, just being jokey.

* * *

OVER THESE DAYS, THE ADULTS HAD STILL NOT MENTIONED the pregnancy, as though this was an adult subject only, not to be shared with children. Did they really think we had not noticed? My mother, her frock in front, pushed to the maximum, making matters clear. To accommodate the new pregnancy, my parents would remain in Becse for the remainder of the summer, to visit friends and such the stated reason, pregnancy being the correct reason. One cannot properly give birth on ships or trains; everyone knows that.

Oma's house now took on all the aspects of an impending birth, the village midwife, experienced in such matters, appearing at our home daily, advising this, suggesting that, in other words, she was getting the job done. And she had a good reputation, yes she had. In our village, doctors were not used for birthing purposes, this being done by midwives. And why not? Even the children of kings were delivered not by the physicians of the day, but by midwives, physicians at the time.

Not fully understanding the need for sanitary measures, the midwives, kitchen trained in cleanliness since the time of the plagues, perhaps without even being aware of it, provided much safer births.

So, Deno was born.

I saw it. With the return of my parents, more room was required and the children were given sleeping quarters in the loft. Well, it is a simple matter to remain awake and peer down to the rooms below, and see what's going on. I watched my mother in labour and was fascinated by it. There were no men present for this. Opa and my father made themselves scarce under the circumstances. And I don't know where they went, to another's house perhaps, to drink wine and discuss the possibilities for the newcomer and at a time where there was no government help or government pensions, the birth of another child, especially a boy, would provide help in retirement. So, each of the men would lift the glass with the hope for a boy, who could work and help provide.

On the other hand, the birth of a girl child could only mean additional family sacrifice, needing even to muster a dowry upon marriage, costs going up.

My father got lucky. The birth was a boy.

THE MONTHS WENT BY. DENO, THANKS BE TO GOD, was healthy, not like me, born sickly and the runt of the litter; so small was I, fitting into the palm of my father's hand looking like a little piglet. Lucky for all of us, Deno was big and solid.

Preparations for leaving for the New World were being made. Three steamer trunks showed up, new ones, paid for by Oma and

Opa for the dreaded occasion, the dreaded leaving. A situation made worse by the artificial cheerfulness that everyone was displaying. Even I started faking it, to say it was okay, that it would all be for the best. Simply, I was all tired out. Tired of feeling like I was dying inside, my heart thoroughly broken, all hope abandoned. I had to speak to myself, convince myself that there could be no other possible outcome, to tell myself to accept the inevitable.

Opa harnessed the horses, the two geldings and not the two beautiful mares which as you know were stolen by the army. What happens to people when they join the army? Why do they so often become bullies? Does power in hands of the ignorant bring it on?

The night before the leaving, no one got much sleep. This was a time before aeroplanes flew across the Atlantic. Most parents of Becse, when their children left them, knew this was probably the last time they would spend together, the children knowing this is the final time with their parents. It was like a live funeral, with all the dead people in attendance, not in boxes, but alive and hugging each other, feeling desperate, fully aware that this is the end, never to see each other again. You think this is silly of me to say? Well, isn't this the same as a funeral, each not seeing the other ever again? Gone from sight, forever? Gone like the wind?

But then, why do they do it? Why do they abandon the most important things in life, being the people they love? Is it for adventure? Is it for greed? Surely the people of Becse were not living in poverty in those years, just farming of course, but all the necessities of life were available, just not many luxuries. What is it about a luxury that has so much appeal? Is it the rarity of such? Or is it another case of poor people wishing to appear as rich people, not knowing that life for the rich is like a too big meal, complete with all the discomforts. Oma would often say something like that, saying being rich is like overeating, like stuffing too much in, like being a fool of food. And she should know, having been rich once upon a time herself. She would say people who think money can cure all their ills, never really had any.

The three steamer trunks, big as these were, could not contain all the personal items we had assembled to take away. So, we were told to cut it down, eliminate, cast to one side those items considered luxury. Well, I had very few luxuries, so even some of the good stuff had to be cast aside, including my favourite lederhosen given to me by an Austrian cousin. This was a favourite of mine, although my skinny bum and legs hardly filled it, the lederhosen stretched earlier by a much fuller person. This would make Opa to joke that my legs were so skinny that while walking even at a slow pace the lederhosen had to gallop at a high rate of speed just to keep up. Along with a bunch of my bedclothes, the lederhosen got left behind.

The packing is finished. Neighbour Sandor has been helping to load everything onto the wagon, and we all head for the railway. This is November now, with quite a nip in the air, most of the leaves fallen, adding to the melancholy of the moment. Thank God that at least the sun was shining, giving a little cheer.

At the train station, only postmaster Tinodi was present, along with a few school chums of mine, who had heard of the leaving and were kind enough to be here, and happily including the neighbour's boy, the one I stuffed the hot peppers into. He had the good grace to be here, upon my going away to North America.

I was glad to see him, but I could have done very well without the presence of Mr. Tinodi, you can say that again.

Oma had us arrive at the train station fully a half hour ahead of time, the purpose to allow a lingering, stretching the final moments together, a kind of benediction, knowing this would be the last of our history as a European family.

Things were loaded on. The three trunks hunkered down, and

passage tickets distributed all around, pinned to the lapels of each child, for safekeeping, no passage without them.

And we finally said our goodbyes, painful and tearful, and we moved into the passenger car, the parents on one side, the children facing.

Suddenly the train jerked to a start. On the station platform, I could see our neighbour Sandor who had remained to see us off, and standing just in front of him are the two most important people of my life, then as now, Opa and my dear Oma, both attempting to smile, trying to bring us comfort, but with matters now clearly out of their hands.

Such unbearable sadness.

And the train started to move out, chugging to gain speed, and at my window, beside the train, running to keep up, was the neighbour boy, the plum boy, not smiling at all, a serious look on his face, just running as fast as he could, trying to keep up, until the train rounded a bend, putting him out of sight, him being my last recollection of Becse, in the country of Hungary, where I was born.

I have since believed that if I had stayed in Becse I would have married the plum boy. There was something between us, and him running proved it.

Later I was to learn that Oma placed my pyjamas, the ones with the hearts and arrows on it in a drawer among her own clothes, left it unwashed, where it remained until her death.

To say more on this, when she died in 1947, she had lived through still another war, and the death of her true love my Opa, and never was she to see again her daughter my mother, my siblings or me.

 I TRIED TO MAKE THE BEST OF THIS TRIP. THE FIRST leg would be from Becse to Budapest, and then from Budapest to Trieste which is on the Mediterranean, and then by boat onward to Halifax, and finally by rail from Halifax to Simcoe, in the province of Ontario, ending at the big, new farm, one hundred acres, four times bigger than anything in Becse. This was supposed to be the prize.

But, before leaving from Becse, I wanted to know the distances between all these places. I wanted exact measurements. Uncertain about everything else in my life, I wanted some certainty: the distance from here to there, in miles.

I got this information from our school's teacher, Miss Lengyel, who I am sad to say, never much liked me at school even though I was always good with my sums, but seeing my distress, she some how found sympathy, doing her best to answer all these distance questions. Even though not liking me much, still she bothered to obtain the information. This is grace. Not liking, but still giving. May God bless her truly, and if she has passed on, may she receive a special seat in Paradise. Yes, she worked very hard to obtain my information, going through this atlas or that, questioning town's officials, posting the Canadian embassy in Budapest at her own cost, coming up with firm answers. And when she was finished, this is what she gave me, written on a new sheet of school paper, neatly and in her best hand:

Here is the information you asked for.

	(in miles)
From Becse to Budapest by rail	250
From Budapest to Trieste by rail	275
From Trieste to Halifax in Canada, by boat	3,400
From Halifax to Simcoe, the new farm, by rail	715
Total miles	4,640

Good Luck to you and your family on their adventure.
Your grade school teacher, Miss Lengyel.

* * *

WE WERE ABOUT TWO HOURS OUT OF BECSE, AND IT WAS TIME
for our lunch, which went very differently in the presence of my
parents, as compared to when Oma and I had made the same trip
and lunched on the train, a few months earlier. Do you remember
how cheerful we were? Of course, you do. Just Oma and me, the
two of us, laughing and giggling while sharing our humble meal
of fried bread, topped with sour cream and greens, washed down
with a shared bottle of sweet lemonade. Giggling we were, at this
silly thing or that, shushing ourselves if too loud, just having a
pleasant time, no damage done.

Now it was different. My father, the poet, the unhappy
perfectionist, demanded full attention as he began preparation for
our travelling meal. Here he is with his sharp deer knife, cutting
slices of rye bread from the loaf that Oma had placed for us in a
wicker. Now, he cuts each slice into two inch squares, and taking a
pepperoni sausage, cuts wafer thin pieces of the meat, placing one
wafer of pepperoni atop each square of bread, and then giving us
a hard smile, calls these carefully prepared squares of bread and
pepperoni, "horses and riders." This could be amusing enough, but
so careful was he in the cutting, the arranging, the preparation
for eating, that all the fun went out. So then, everything is eaten
in silence, a gloom settling in, each square carefully examined
before being eaten, us kids faking interest in the horses and riders
through forced respect.

My mother saying nothing much, just attending Deno,
the new one.

So, the trip was quickly becoming a dull one. I suppose you
can easily see why I preferred to spend time with my Oma and
Opa, rather than with my mother and father. Can you see how a
person's personality can so affect similar situations? With Oma's
personality, same train trip, lunching is a funful event rather

than a serious thing. And the meeting with other passengers, Oma asking all the right questions, enquiring the state of their lives for goodness sakes. You will of course remember the man with a strange pear-shaped eye pupil, followed by the babushka lady, headed for Budapest to pick up the body of her dead sailor husband. Wasn't that trip interesting? Wasn't that rich?

I have never forgotten these things, and I have reminisced on them many times in my adult life, wishing by magic to be whisked back, returning to my early childhood, and the fun of it, and life with Oma and Opa.

Breaking the silence I said, " This is a pleasant train trip, much as when Oma and I travelled this route last May."

"What travel, what?" said my father. It was occurring to me now, that Oma had not told him about her trip to Budapest. And if Oma had not told him, perhaps there was a reason not to, but having started this revelation there was no way for me to back up, once a thing is said, it can't be unsaid, I have always been aware of that. But he was waiting for an answer, looking directly at me. So, I continued with, "Well, Oma and I did this very same thing, I believe it was last May or so, she and I went to Budapest."

"Why would she have done that?" said my father, "She has not done that in years. So why would she go. Tell me that one."

"She went to visit her sisters."

"That's even more silly. She has no interest in her sisters, the lavish ones, in Budapest. She would not do that. So you must be lying, not telling the truth, being childish."

Anyone who knows me, then as now, is aware that it is not in my nature to suffer unfair accusations, not even from a father, so I said, "She went to borrow money."

"Fiction!" said my father, "Your Oma is not a borrower. She would never do such a thing."

Now he was making me angry, him being so judgmental. So, then I fully let the cat out the bag by saying, "She went to her sisters to borrow money. Money for you. You needed the money. You were broke in Canada. She did it for you!"

"Nonsense! Saying such stuff."

Now I would not be stopped, "And she needed to sell the household cow too! She sold Mully, our Jersey. The best cow! The one for market products! She sold her to get this money, because you needed it. And on top, borrowed from her sisters."

Clear, he was beginning to believe me. I had him buffaloed. I had shut him down. I was simply giving too much accurate detail to be considered a liar. And it shocked him. Made him feel small, him not even asking what he owed Oma, when he had a chance back in Becse, and so to at least discuss the possibility of repayment. Or even award simple thanks, under the circumstances. The weight of this was dawning on him.

"Well, she will be repaid, you can be certain of that," he said. "There will be much money made with a full one hundred acres in Simcoe. Don't worry. What she gave will come back to her."

That was simply big talk and nothing else. And little did my father realize that within two years of this speech to me, things would get even worse and he would become financially bankrupt, lose his one hundred acre farm in Simcoe, impoverish his young family in a foreign country, and suddenly die under mysterious circumstances.

All that was still to come.

AS WE APPROACHED BUDAPEST I WOULD POINT OUT to my father this landmark or that, having been here before, much to his annoyance, him wishing to be exclusive narrator, I think. But I am always willing to throw in my two cents worth, and I carried on with this while new passenger cars were added to the train to accommodate the increasing numbers of passengers taking the trip westward towards Trieste and the Adriatic Sea. Most of those boarding were heading for North America.

As the train moved west, mountains such height I had never seen before rose in the distance. My father, pointing out this elevation or that, in that poetic way of his, switching from low Hungarian, the dialect of the rurals, to high Hungarian, the language of the studying classes, describing the mountains before us, how beautiful they are, how rare and precious is God's special handiwork, creating these mountains.

Well, I jumped in to say, as beautiful as these mountains are, the plains of Hungary, the flatlands, the land of where Becse is, has a beauty too. Their beauty, I said, is one of foodstuffs, producing food for the nation and the mountains here, beautiful yes, but just something to look at, unfarmable, clearly a case of beauty and no substance. At this remark, after some pause, my father merely leaned back in his seat, folded his hands on his lap, moved his eyes to the ceiling, and gave a sigh, suggesting that nothing I said could be meaningful, in other words, "I am leaving now, no point in baiting the child."

Well, let him have his idea on the matter. He is wrong again. Wrong like so many times in his life, this being just one time, more.

The day wore on and this trip was tiring each of us. With no sleeping accommodations in the passenger car, we slept as best we could, in shifts perhaps, my father dozing, my mother not at all, each time I awakened, she would still be there, the infant beside her, or on her lap, or her chest, and she would be fully awake. And I began to wonder, time playing tricks, was this the same day? The same day we left. Or was this tomorrow. Or even midweek. I had been in and out of sleep so often, the car dark and then light, returning to dark again that I began to lose perception. Although I was able to tell time, there was no clock in the railcar, and I would not ask my father for the time since he would make such an issue of it, reaching for his gold fob, pulling the chain until the watch became revealed, and then peering down at the face, quizzically first, a wrinkle to the brow as though a big deal in the offing, and then finally announce the correct time, if a please and thank you was tendered first.

Well, no thanks to all that rigmarole.

But my payment for stubbornness in not asking, was to become day-confused, made worse by the fatigue of the long trip, the constant sideways shifting of the railcar as it covered the tracks, my legs becoming as rubber from all this sitting and all this motion, me weaving as a village drunk whenever allowed to walk the length of the railcar for exercise, and then the adults' heads slowly turning, scrutinizing me as I strolled, them being on the watch for bad behaviour.

And I remember that I was becoming thoroughly hungry. The horses and riders, the wafers of rye bread and pepperoni were long gone, and we were into simple bread now, not even buttered, the lemonade and even ordinary water having run out, too.

I have always thought it amazing, how the sight of a familiar object can make you reminisce. Seemingly, the mind needs a starting point, some central focus. So now, me looking at the near empty wicker basket my Oma had prepared for us, my eyes filled with tears, me thinking that if Oma knew we were hungry now, not enough food, she would be appalled. She would feel that she had failed, putting in less than we needed. But how was she to know? How could she know the correct amount for a trip so long? But she would be appalled, oh yes, she would.

Hunger produces stomach discomforts. There was now a real pain in my belly, coming up with gases that I dare not release, my father sitting opposite, so I tried to control all this, squeezing my cheeks together. All this was very tiring. I tried to sleep and entering a relaxed state I unknowingly gave a fart, and immediately became aware of it, a horrible transgression, trying now to wish it away, squeezing my brow and keeping my eyes shut in the foolish belief that if I did not see him now sitting across from me, he could not criticize. Please, no criticism. I had done my best.

There was no sound from him.

So I stayed in a relaxed state. I dozed off now. To fill the time hanging heavy, I allowed my imagination to take over, and in my mind's eye I saw our train not westbound, but by mistake, hooked by the train master to the wrong engine in Budapest, we were headed south now, back to Becse. Back to Becse! Hallelujah! A blessing from God! Our train incorrectly hooked! We were headed home! No longer heading toward Trieste and the Adriatic Sea, we are here, arriving home now, and there is Oma! Opa too! Both waving hello to us, welcoming us back. And yes, as to be expected, there is postmaster Tinodi standing with the greeting party, bidding us a welcome. Everyone glad to see us.

And a meal is prepared. What a meal this is! Not of silly horse and pepperoni riders, but a full meal, a welcomed meal, rich in sauces, a terrific green sorrel salad, and the yeasty taste of potato biscuits. And finally! Yes, finally! The meal is topped off with two cottage cheese blintzes, these finished in the oven, brown sugar melting on top from the heat, and a few blueberries sprinkled just for decoration.

A child's mind can do this. A child can create improved circumstances, wishing away the bad and welcoming the good. It's an ability given to them to help them through childhood. It is something I needed to do as a child, from time to time.

Perhaps, it was the same with you.

16 HERE COMES TRIESTE! HERE COMES TRIESTE! IT WAS my sister Hanna calling down the car having been given an exercise period, and overhearing from adults that Trieste was in the horizon.

Well, Trieste or not, I was still hungry. I have been told, and perhaps it is true, that starvation is painless. Hunger is painful but starvation is not, because acidic potions in the stomach produce a natural anaesthesia and the pain disappears and if that was the case, I wasn't starving to death, the pain being plentiful, but I was indeed, hungry. A hunger such as I had never felt before. Can you imagine in your own life, looking down into a stranger's quart glass bottle containing floating frankfurter pieces, and wanting it? Just *wanting* it? How lucky is this owner of this jar! Well, that's exactly what I was experiencing as the train approached the port city of Trieste. I had spotted a lady with a jar on her lap filled with frankfurter pieces, little German sausages floating in a brine of vinegar and onion water. And I asked her for some.

My father was elsewhere at the time, probably at the front of the car, straining for a sight of Trieste.

So, she gave. Seeing my hunger she offered two pieces, telling me to eat them slowly, not to gobble lest I become sick, if I was truly hungry. I did as she told, because I immediately trusted her, she being so generous under the circumstances, offering me these frankfurter pieces, the delicious ones.

Could I ask her for some more? Could I ask for a piece for Bela and Klara and Hanna? Would that be proper? As I began to search for a way to do this, my father suddenly reappeared, bringing all activities to a halt.

"Get back to our seats," is what I heard. "We will be boarding our ship, the *Belvedere*, at 13:00 hrs this afternoon. There will be supper there. No need to go borrowing food from other passengers. You have no shame."

He had seen what I had done.

THE BOARDING OF THE *BELVEDERE*, OUR SHIP, WAS not a glamorous affair. There were no bands making music or relatives waving from the embayment as seen in newsreels. That's because the *Belvedere* was anchored away from shore, rumours flowing that leftover explosive mines are in the harbour, so the ship stayed out, a smaller ferryboat taking passengers to the ship.

Well okay, cheaper to have a ferryboat blow up than a huge steamship! Proving once again how silly the business of war is, these mines we are trying to avoid are Italian mines, placed during the war by Italians, and now an Italian steamship, the *Belvedere*, is in danger of being blown up by leftover Italian mines placed in a harmful way, by their own selves! Stupidity, as my Oma would declare, perfect stupidity. Not just *ordinary* stupidity, she would say, of which there is a plentiful supply, but *perfect* stupidity, carefully studied almost like art, made perfect.

I was greatly impressed by the *Belvedere*, although by marine standards she was not a big ship, about half the size of important ships, and chosen by my parents more for price than for comfort, the bigger ships better in high seas, these smaller ships, coming out strong on pricing, but rolling even in calm waters. Small or not, I was impressed. You must bear in mind that this was the first steamship that I had ever seen in my young life. My Becse is a landlocked town, no large lakes, just the river. So this ship looked immense, especially while being transported to it by ferryboat, approaching the hull, huge appeared, but I was not frightened, indeed, by this time I was looking forward to the journey across the Atlantic, the trip now becoming more important to me. In my mind's eye, I can still see the impressive smoke stack, a red funnel it was, with black top, and a broad white band on the red, and presenting puffs of white smoke coming up like you see in *LIFE* magazine.

So, for the rest of the afternoon, all the passengers, well over a thousand people, were ferried to the ship, young families, some with a dozen kids, coming up. And once aboard the ship, we Third Class passengers were assembled in a great hall, to be given a lesson by the captain, translated into several languages, on ship's etiquette, what to do, what not to do.

Third Class passengers (that's us):	1,260
Second Class passengers:	140
First Class passengers:	only 12

Now the captain began. "There are twelve very important First Class Passengers aboard this ship," says the Captain, "and you who are travelling Third Class, well, you are to stay on Deck C well away from the First Class Passengers no matter what the circumstance. Very important. Their comfort is of the greatest meaning and you, the Third Class passengers, of which there are the greatest number, you thousand can do much to make this trip pleasant for them."

A small buzz began among us. How to give the twelve First Class passengers a feeling of pleasantness? How to do this? Well, we thought, perhaps by saying good morning, giving a broad smile, in a chanced meeting while walking. Or, perhaps the twelve First Class Passengers could be made more comfortable by Third Class passengers if we willingly offered our deck chair, jumping up immediately, bidding them to seat themselves, here, make yourself comfortable, have a chair. Or perhaps we could share familial stories with them, speaking to them in an informal manner. Would that do it?

"No," said the captain. "By staying away."

Not going to be easy for me, since as you know, Oma would say I am as quick as a spark off a fire. Even before this meeting on ship's etiquette, having arrived just hours earlier, I had already been through all three decks, at one point pressing my face against the *Belvedere*'s steel hull now below the waterline, feeling the coldness of the Adriatic waters on my cheek, and then down to the engine rooms, strictly off limits and into the kitchen I go, making the Sardinian cooks laugh at my colossal nerve, them giving me a free bite of this or that, just having a thoroughly good time.

That's how it went. And in the excitement of the moment, thoughts of my Oma and Opa quickly disappear.

Tug boats take us out of the harbour and into the sea. Now they cast off and our mighty engines fire up. The vibration, the sounds heard now for the first time, would continue for the next eleven days, day and night, without stop, pulling us through all the storms of the winter Atlantic, still to come.

I do not care much for Italian food. Sorry to hurt some feelings, but tomato sauce is no substitute for high quality paprika, which appears in most Hungarian foods. As a matter of fact, there are those who criticize Hungarian cuisine, saying there is a kind of sameness, with paprika as king. Well, it isn't just the paprika. To a skilled Hungarian palate, it is also, the amount of paprika, this being varied for different dishes, the subtlety in one case, intensity in another. Sure, the amount of paprika used is crucial. Well, there is no paprika in Italian food aboard an Italian ship with a Sardinian kitchen. None. Even this first evening meal, just low grade noodles with tomato sauce is the fare, topped off with heavy mugs of tea with canned milk. And I am under pressure from my father to eat up, him always saying how skinny I am, so bony, like a sparrow.

Well, people should know, some of us fill up quickly, that's the only answer. My need for food was always for a little.

Travelling accommodations were unusual. My father was required to share a bunk with the service crew, and my mother and my other siblings, plus two other women, shared a separate cabin, because in Third Class, there were many arrangements, in some cases even utilizing cargo space.

That night, that first night, I fell to sleep very fast. Just too much had happened on this day and I needed to get away from it all. Sleep filled the bill.

ON THIS TRIP MY SISTERS AND BROTHER STAYED close to my parents, but I have always been very social so it didn't take long for me to find a friend on the ship, turning out to be a member of the crew, an Albanian boy of twenty years, known as Vangjush Tashco, whose name I shortened to Vanny, just for convenience. He started out as a cabin boy, he said, and just recently was given the responsibility of a sailor, which meant getting paid for his work, cabin boys getting no pay, just a place on the ship, giving service to the crew, getting this, getting that, just a fetcher.

He was dark in complexion, quite tall, taller than most Albanians, and he was full of mischief, which made him very interesting to me, always bending the rules, if not completely breaking them. So he proved to be a fast friend, especially since he was able to speak serviceable Hungarian, me not knowing any Albanian, and just a very little English. And sure enough, just like the Serbian soldier in Becse, it wasn't long before he had me riding on his shoulders, carrying me around on deck, pretending to stumble, having me to fall forward, and then catching me just as I was to break loose, scaring the dickens out of me, making a ruckus.

And he was full of information. For example, first day out to sea, many were sick, especially the twelve First Class passengers, puking over the rails, etc., etc. The Second Class passengers had a few sick, but certainly not one hundred percent like the First Class passengers. And Third Class, that's us, had the fewest, just about a dozen, including my mother.

So, I said to Vanny, "Why are the twelve rich persons in First Class puking so much?" Vanny said, with a wise look in his eye, "It's because they have the best cabins."

"Huh?"

"Sure. The First Class passengers are on Deck A, the top of the ship, affording the best views. But the greatest movement, the most pitch and yaw, is occurring at the highest point of the ship above the water, the least is at the waterline. It's the pitch and yaw that makes one puke. And because Third Class is below the waterline there is almost none."

"And less puking," I jumped in with.

"Exactly," said Vanny. "If you want to avoid being seasick just stay below the waterline and close to the middle of the ship, which they can't do in First Class because their cabins are at the top to present the best views."

Wow. Vanny knew everything.

Now, it was the second day out. We had left the Adriatic Sea, our ship floating majestically, even if smaller than some of the others, and stopping at a port in Sicily to pick up a cargo of figs and dates for export. Now, headed through the Mediterranean.

"There it is!" I was yelling to Vanny one bright and sunny morning, "The Rock of Gibraltar."

"No," said Vanny, "It's the White Cliffs of Dover."

"You shitter Vanny! The White Cliffs of Dover are in the English Channel, I learned that from Miss Lengyel at school. This is the Mediterranean."

Vanny gave me a hug. Not a romantic hug, no, nothing as that, nothing that could be considered unwanted interference. A boy like Vanny would never give you unwanted interference. I was told about such a thing by my Oma, how to spot it, why it happens, why a little girl should avoid young men if they present themselves in a certain way. So, I say in confidence, those hugs from Vanny were never wrongly intended, just nice hugs, making us both to feel good, a very pleasant thing making us to feel closer.

Well, the fact is, just give me a hug, and you have won me over.

One day, I said to Vanny, "Gee, I'm getting tired of these Italian foods, it would be nice to taste something that hasn't got a tomato in it."

You need to know that the fare really wasn't very good on the *Belvedere*, especially for Third Class passengers such as we were. Well, think about it. There were over one thousand of us Third Classers. That would mean making one thousand breakfasts every day, one thousand lunches every day, one thousand suppers every day. The easiest way to get over that one, the Sardinian cooks figured, was to boil noodles and top it off with tomato sauce. Or anyway, as one steward said, "You will be on the water for twelve days only, all we need to do is to keep you alive. Noodles and sauce will do it."

Second class had better fare but not by much, Vanny telling me they threw in a few sausages along with the sauce.

"First Class, now that is good fare," said Vanny. "Those who get to eat with the captain get the good stuff. Always been that way. The tradition of the sea puts the best food on the captain's table, and the First Class passengers share in it." "Well" I said, "will you get me one of those sausages?"

"I'll do better than that," said Vanny, "I'll get a place for you at the captain's table.

"Really? But I am not properly dressed for the first class diner," I said.

"Well, don't worry about it. Just wear your mauve frock. You look terrific in your mauve frock. That's a nice one."

I should also say, it was not an easy task to keep my father satisfied regarding my whereabouts each day. I needed to check into Deck C at regular times, to let them know of my whereabouts, me pretending just to enjoy wandering, them being satisfied that since this was a ship, I could not go too far, and my wandering made it one less child to need to deal with, my sisters and brother, plus the infant taking up much of their time.

But to dine at the Captain's table! I could hardly wait. What would be on the plates? Huge pieces of roast beef perhaps? Maybe.

Here I am, near the dinner hour, outside the Deck C diner, and here comes my hero, Vanny, whistling an Albanian tune, and while still walking, grabbing me by the hand taking me up to First Class, Deck A, to the diner, all the tables seating just four people, not crowded like ours was, and tablecloths and glasses with a napkin tucked in each, and then Vanny switching to Italian, saying, this little girl lost her mother and father in Hungary, dying of a blood disorder, and she was shipping to Halifax to live with an uncle and aunt. Just lying about it, giving me details later. What a liar, that Vanny! Making up a big story. Well, suddenly the First Class passengers are very sympathetic, one lady from Venezia bidding me, please to sit with her, it would be a pleasure. Well as it turns out, it was a good thing I could not speak Italian, making it unnecessary to carry on a conversation with the Venezia lady about my dear departed mother and father, and whether I have brothers and sisters, and who is my uncle. Just to enjoy all the good things from the captain's table, which I did.

But that's my Vanny. Always up to something.

19   TRAVELLING OUT TO SEA, LEAVING LAND BEHIND, the *Belvedere*'s powerful engines are humming, churning up the Atlantic, beating against the waves, leaving a turquoise wake behind, with white tips and a spray that sometimes hit as high as the sky. I was excited. We were heading for North America, I had found a good friend aboard ship and I was inventing adventures, stealing away to First Class, sunning myself on those shiny deck chairs, sometimes reading my little white Communion Bible, since I had little else to read, but it made me an unexpected hit with some of the First Class passengers. How spiritual must that little girl be! How wonderful! Goodness gracious! Well, to be truthful I might have read something else, given a choice. But, the Good Book served me well aboard that ship, and in later years too, since much of the English I speak

now, came from reading the King James in English, studying the text, coming up with understanding. And as an extra benefit in sad times still to come, I would find strength in such passages as found in Psalm 86. If ever you find your life coming apart, I would recommend it for your reading.

We were three days out when a terrible storm hit. It started out slowly first, just the good ship *Belvedere* gently slapping on waves. Before very long, we were given the message to stay in our quarters and remain calm. Remain calm? Why? What was that one all about?

The reason became clear. In just a short time, the ship was not just gently slapping on the waves, now she was banging on the surface of the water. And the banging got louder, and soon you could slip off your chair, so pronounced was the motion of the ship and the severity of the banging. Her bow would lift higher and higher and then go banging down into the depths of the waves. Sometimes the back of the ship was so high into the night air, the propellers reflecting in the bright deck lights would start to race— whrrrrrr! Whrrrrrrrr! Whrrrrrr!—indicating that the ship was no longer churning water, her propellers were spinning in the air, her engines being played for a fool. And just when I thought this could not get worse, it did, now with a side motion becoming apparent; not only were we were going up and down, the boat was going sideways too, making no forward progress. Locked in a huge valley of water we were, the *Belvedere* stalled in the mid-Atlantic, in the basin of a huge wave.

We were given towels to vomit in.

And I thought to myself. Are people crazy? Are we each nuts? Coming out into a ferocious winter sea like this, the *Belvedere* a tiny bauble on the surface of the water? We could break in half! Indeed, it has happened. Ships have broken into two pieces, just getting tired of a tremendous beating served up by a riled sea. Could you blame her if she broke into two pieces under these circumstances? And if she broke, she should not be faulted, for it is we who take her out, causing her to challenge the mighty ocean, courting disaster as they say, "challenging Neptune," for goodness sakes.

Yes, purposely challenging Neptune! Neptune, that mighty god of the sea, son of Saturn, brother to Jupiter! How could we dare to challenge the private domain of such a powerful figure, him with such high connections and we with a tiny boat, a 7,000 ton ship, 418 feet long, one funnel, two masts, over a thousand sorry souls aboard. Oh yes, oh yes, a very small ship compared with others such as the *Laconia* of the Cunard line, bigger than the *Belvedere* by twice, weighting 20,000 tons, plying the seas in such confidence emboldened by a huge size. Or the *Lusitania*, three times as large as the *Belvedere*, weighting 30,000 tons but later sent to a watery grave by a German U-boat torpedo. Or the *Titanic*, everyone heard of that one, weighting 46,000 tons, being four and a half times as large as our ship and then making unfortunate contact with a piece of floating glacier, sinking in just three hours, gone to the bottom.

But here she is, the *Belvedere*, banging up and down on the surface of the Atlantic, taking terrible punishment. Later, Vanny told me that the captain did not believe the ship would survive on that night, the waves just too powerful, the ship too small— she was taking on water and the bilge pumps could hardly do the job. But even against such unfair odds, she did not break into pieces as many might. The *Belvedere* was a terrific ship. Some say the composition of her metal was responsible for her survival, being not brittle, stretching just a little under pressure rather than snapping like a dry twig, unlike the *Titanic* whose hull was brittle like glass, I have read, breaking under pressure, turning to smithereens. But the *Belvedere* eventually did sink. The story is that she was scuttled by her owners, sold and sunk for the ignoble purpose of shoring up a harbour on the French coast, her owners squeezing the last few dollars out of her, selling her as a breakwater on the bottom of the sea for goodness sakes. Our brave ship, that beautiful *Belvedere*, sunk for a few dollars for those who owned her, too small to profit under modern conditions, she was simply cashed in, sunk to the bottom of a harbour, her plug pulled, a gallant ship gone.

Ship owners care not a tinker's damn about their ships beyond the level of profit. Seldom do they even see their fleet except by artist's renderings each hung neatly in a row on office walls. Look, I got twelve of them.

Are these amazing vessels just entries in a ledger? And if that is the case, please tell me, where might I find the dignity of that?

20

"WHEN WE GET TO HALIFAX, WHAT CAN I expect?" I was speaking to Vanny now, he who knows everything, Mr. Expert in other words. Or maybe not an expert, perhaps a generalist, or maybe an expert and a generalist, if it is possible to be both, and in his case it might be, him being so darned smart. Because we would be approaching the coast of Canada within two days, I wanted to know what it would look like, what would come up as a lasting impression, the first sight.

"Is there a statue, a statue like the American one, a statue of Liberty?" I asked, "Is there a symbol first to be seen on the coast of Canada, welcoming us perhaps?"

"No," said Vanny, "Canada is a humbler country than the United States. It doesn't have a statue at the harbour, it doesn't have a lot of symbols, not even its own flag, using the Union Jack of Britain instead, and it has a King borrowed from England, but except for the use of a King, it is a similar country to the U.S. of America, similar but still different."

"I wonder Vanny," I said now with a child's endless curiosity, "how something could be similar, but different. Isn't similar different? Can a thing be similar, and still be different? In that case, how different could it be until it lost its similarity? Would that mean that its difference would be so little as to become meaningless? Meaning almost the same but not quite?"

"Exactly," said Vanny, "Now you got it."

I was so relieved with this assurance. Because I know in Becse many families left our little town, choosing the U.S.A. instead of Canada, supposing the U.S. to be better. And so with this assurance from Vanny, I was pleased to know that going to Canada was to be an equally good choice. My family chose Canada first, as you know, because of Count Esterhazy recruiting Hungarian families to fill the town in Saskatchewan named in his honour. Well, you could be certain if the United States offered him a town in Kansas, that would have filled the bill, too, the Count's proudness needing to be satisfied, nothing more. And anyway, it was my father who put us here, in wanting the chance to create riding boots for the Northwest Mounted Police. And his wish to spend as much time with a boot as might be necessary. Not the cobbling of boots, but the creation of art. And then later, him becoming disappointed with the leathers given him to work with, not up to snuff, finally cancelling the whole matter, saying what's the point, nobody knows what's good.

But my father always lived with disappointment. With him there was always an air of displeasure. He would quietly shrug his shoulders at this result or that, things always falling short of his highest standard. Too much a poet perhaps was he, in a practical setting, making it difficult for him.

But why did God put poets here on earth, anyway? They cannot be satisfied, these people seeking only ideals, everything ideal, the need for all things perfect. I have some of that characteristic in me too, but I fight it, knowing its destructive qualities, and I fight with the realization that everything here on earth is a little on the foolish side, that things are never what they seem, that birth is death delayed, and we better make the best of what we have here, not much in the cup.

But strangely, it's the work of the poets which is most remembered.

21   A THIN, BLACK LINE ON THE HORIZON!

It was coming into view. Canada in the distance, bringing much excitement aboard the Belvedere. Those of us seeing it for the first time, what a thrill!

"Vanny! This is it! That's Canada, isn't it?"

Vanny was pleased for me. Pleased to see the excitement that this event was bringing to me. He smiled, and hugged me, and it did not occur to me at the time, but this was the last hug I would receive from Vanny, my friend, my ten-day wonder, who I felt I had known all my life, in just ten days. I have thought much about this. To this day. Where is Vanny now? What happened to him? Did he marry someone? Did he live a long life? Is he still on the sea? Did he always remain so happy? It is unfair, to be lucky enough in knowing another person so completely, delighting even at the sight of him, knowing him so well in so short a time, and then to have him disappear, like it didn't happen in the first place, like a whimsy.

There is something very unfair in that.

Now the thin black line on the horizon begins to broaden and to take up colours of green and brown, beginning to appear alive. Pieces of towns are coming into view and finally the Canadian city of Halifax appears, presenting many boats of every size. Our engines shut down as we entered the harbour, and that was a shock, too. We had been living with the constant buzzing of the engines for almost two weeks, and now with them silenced, there was an awkward quiet, just the gentle rocking of the Belvedere back and forth on the calm waters of the harbour.

Men's voices were heard now, clearly, as we took on a pilot for the final docking, a tug boat preparing to pull the ship into her berth. The gangplank was extended, and the passengers began to file off into the customs and immigration section to verify passports and visas, completing government's business, our luggage to be later unloaded.

On the dock now, I suddenly realized that I had walked away from Vanny without saying goodbye. I was so taken up with events. Now, I could not see him. I looked up to the upper deck. No, he was not there. Looking up, I scanned every face I could see aboard the *Belvedere*, from the stem to the stern, and none was his. I did so a second time, still nothing. I lingered hoping by luck to see him, to give him a wave, just to once more see him. My family is starting to walk ahead of me.

My father turns to me and says, "Come on now! You're being tardy. Hurry up! We have to go through the customs together, not separately. They have rules to obey here."

He was nervous.

IN THE CUSTOMS OFFICE, PROBLEMS WERE cropping up. The name on my official papers was different than my family name, a mixup to be sure, but after much investigation, and questioning, the customs agent agreed that I was indeed, "a daughter to this father, and someone "over there" said the agent, meaning Hungary, "must be dull at his job." My father was preparing to respond to this minor insult, I could see it in his eyes, but then giving second thought, troubles enough, he kept silent.

Now the custom agent turns to my sister Klara and another problem comes up. Remember that sore on her upper arm that my sister Klara always had? Well, listen to this: that sore on her arm was another incident almost cancelling our entry into Canada, the customs man spotting the sore, redness on her upper arm, asking about it, saying, "What is this all about?" At that time, Canada wanted only healthy immigrants since there were no social programmes as there are today, or support given to families. You were on your own from day one, so you needed to be healthy.

"Who is this one? Is this your daughter, too?"

My father nodded his head, wondering again what's up. "Yes, she is my daughter Klara and she is a very good child."

"Where did she get this serious infection?"

"Well, it is not serious, she has always had it," my father said. "It comes and goes. For most of the year she has a clear arm, but it seems when she gets riled, such as from this trip, it sets up a reaction."

"I'm afraid we will need to have a doctor judge it," said the official, "It might be a communicable disease like syphilis or something. We don't want diseases coming into Canada from other countries."

My father's face was reddening. To suggest the presence of a dreaded social disease in his daughter was powerful. This family, his family, had none of that, no messing around going on here, not even alcohol consumption, straight shooters, this bunch.

"What are you talking about? What are you saying? What's the matter with you? She is a child with a sore, nothing more. You talking of syphilis? The people of Becse are not of that kind. There is only good behaviour by its townspeople, there has never been a report about the disease you are thinking about, ask anyone."

Well clearly, there was no one to ask. Here we are in the customs and immigration offices, wire mesh on the windows, the smell of Lysol everywhere, and it is beginning to look as though we were going to be shipped back to Hungary, resulting from my father smart-talking this immigration official.

So, things were looking bad. We were taken away to an anteroom, and made to wait, each of us becoming more anxious, sitting all in a row on a bench, a sorry looking European family we were, confused by circumstances, wondering what's coming up next.

My father, speaking in low tones now, in Hungarian and to himself mostly, saying such as, "How foul can this man be, saying things such as syphilis to a child, in her presence even, not even in private, unspeakable behaviour, rude, crude, where is his politeness, where is his standard of behaviour, what kind of a thinker is he? Well, I am going to complain to the medical doctor about him when he comes in, you can be sure about that one. This kind of speech to a child is inappropriate, not to be tolerated from this ignoramus, him having the ups."

The day became very long. We had to wait until three in the afternoon, until the immigration physician would make his rounds, passing judgment on this one or that, and sometimes closing the gate forever on those whose illnesses are forbidden. Hours of waiting. My father insisting that we remain seated. No wandering. No walking around. He would not even allow me, knees crossed, to rock my leg back and forth, relieving some of the stored up energy. I was ready to burst. My skinny bum, no flesh on it, was not a good cushion, and I needed to slowly place my weight on one cheek for ten minutes or so, switching to the other when the discomfort presented, my sister Klara, her fat bum providing plenty of comfort, sitting pretty.

You will have noticed that my father seems always to attract misery. Never was there a sad situation that he couldn't make worse. Bad enough that we were quarantined like this, now he intended to challenge the authorities, squeal to the doctor about the immigration agent, make a ruckus.

Eventually the doctor came in and I will name him the Sniffer. Because that's what he did while he talked to you. He sniffed, continuous. Barely could he utter a sentence without another sniff being heard.

"Hmmmm. Is this (sniff, sniff) family #BT893? I have a yellow sheet here requesting a physical (sniff) examination of Klara #BT893. What city are you from in Hungary? Budapest I hope. As a foreign student, I was fortunate enough to attend university there (sniff). How is the old town? Doing well? I was attracted to its cultural life. Very good. People talk about Paris as the City of Light, but I would certainly put Budapest in that category (sniff). So, from Budapest?"

"No," said my father. "We are from Becse, a town in the southern part, near Yugoslavia. With Budapest I am very familiar though, many of my friends being there in the arts. My own personal interest, of course, is the poetry of János Arany, who as you might know was a famous Pest citizen and a poet."

"Yes" said the doctor, "I noticed in living there, that the arts are simply taken for granted, everyone interested, an everyday thing."

Now, my father cleared his throat, his eyes to the ceiling, he began to quote from memory the epic poem *Az elveszett alkotmány*, which is a solid mixture of love and patriotism, and about a half hour long. This was recited in Hungarian, and the good doctor, with only limited knowledge of the language, obediently waiting for the lengthy poem to end. When it did, he gave congratulations to my father, saying the commission of such a long and artful poem to memory would indicate a love for the work that must be respected. "You are a remarkable man (sniff, sniff) and a talented presenter. I thank you for the recitation, and I regret there is no way for me to repay you."

My father became daring. He said, "Well, you could repay by helping me through the immigration process here ..." and then he finished the request in High Hungarian, the dialect of the Budapestian, the doctor thoroughly impressed, took a very deep breath, staring forward. So, to express his thanks in an almost embarrassed way, the doctor gave Klara's arm a cursory examination, wrote a few comments on the yellow paper, passed it on to my father, and wished us god speed to our destination in Ontario.

While we were walking to claim our luggage, and to make him feel good about things, I said to my father that the doctor was highly impressed with the recitation of *Az elveszett alkotmány*.

"He's a dope," said my father. "The poem speaks about foolish governmental bureaucrats toying with people's lives, and making a mess of it. In other words, the poem made sport of him, and he didn't even recognize the condemnation. Well, compliments from a low-end intellectual like that have no value. Absolutely. When it comes to the arts, he is just a duffer."

23 FROM HALIFAX, OUR PORT OF ENTRY, TO SIMCOE, to our new home, is about a thousand miles by rail. Our family was loaded on to what they called the Immigrant Trains, or in some cases called the Colonial Trains. Well, whether Immigrant or Colonial, for most Europeans this was a rude experience now into cold weather, the windows of the cars kept closed to contain the heat from a coal stove at each end of the car, and the smell of diapers and of tired, unbathed persons is everywhere. Thinking about it now, perhaps even the great storm on the ocean was an easier experience than this trip on the train.

Oh, I am just joking.

To add to our problems we were again into a shortage of food. Before boarding the train at Halifax harbour, there were vendors, but the food was just meatball sandwiches, the meatball squeezed flat with too much tomato sauce left on, making the white bread soggy. Well, that's what my father collected for us, anyway. Figuring a two-day trip on the train, figuring a meatball sandwich for breakfast, dinner and supper, figuring the six of us, the baby still on mother's milk, my father had gathered twenty-six meatball sandwiches for the trip, which was very wrong, thirty-six should have been the correct amount, proving how weak my father was with sums; well he is a poet, what can you expect. Oh yes, I almost forgot, there were Coca Colas too, but they were provided for free by the Coca Cola company. This was the first Coca Cola I had ever tasted, and I thought it was pretty darn good. However I was not accustomed to anything this sweet since most Hungarian fare, even desserts, are quite dry; the sugar in the Coca Cola riled my stomach, bringing on the belches, releasing of which is hard to do silently, but I had to let them go, pretending to visit the end of the car to warm myself, releasing myself at almost every step along the way in walking to the car's end, some adults giving me the fish eye on hearing the rudeness.

And plus, the Coca Colas brought on a need to pee, which had to be held until the chance was made available at some of the stops along the way, some of which I missed since they were announced by the conductors as "rest stops." And I would think, why stopping for resting? We don't need a rest. We've been sitting. We haven't been doing anything, for goodness sakes! A rest is the last thing we need. Well, it was only later that I learned "rest stop" meant a chance to go to a latrine. That was it! A "rest stop" was a chance to pee in a "rest room." It took a little while for me to catch on. Can you see how difficult it is for a foreigner to learn the English language, with many English words serving two purposes? Of course you can.

Now the train was stopping less often as the towns were farther apart. Hard to believe but even the stopping and starting of a train can promote the interest. The slowing down, the faces of those waiting at the station for loved ones or seeing them off can often add interest. Once the train is on the way, nothing. And I kept looking out the window, looking for Indians, residents of Canada as told to me at school by Miss Lengyel, and to my disappointment there were none. I was expecting to see a Chief of

Indians sitting there on his horse, without a saddle, magnificent in his huge feathered headdress, his horse waiting earnestly beneath him, ready to spring forward and chase the buffaloes.

Well, there were no Indians. No buffaloes. Just small dreary towns, but as the train approached Quebec City, at least there was a huge hotel to be seen, which was the Frontenac and that was a good one. Later with the train approaching Montreal, I could see tall office buildings, nothing this tall in Budapest, in old Europe no buildings were allowed to be built higher than the king's palace. A big rule to be taken seriously. Now it is different. Few kings are left. They went with the dodos.

Now, there is a two-hour holdover in Montreal, which is not welcomed at all. Later, it was told that the train was held up for a visiting dignitary, a person of political importance, but I can't even remember his name, that's how important he was. But, there you go.

After the holdover, the train ambled down along the mighty St. Lawrence River. I wanted to see the St. Lawrence River in full, but I was only offered quick moments of it since the train tracks ran somewhat inland, connecting the towns together, such as Cornwall, Brockville, Belleville, Kingston. And I said, to myself, why is this? Why cannot I see the mighty St. Lawrence as I had remembered seeing it on the map in our little schoolhouse in Becse? I know the river is there, to my left as I travel. But why am I given just fleeting moments of it. Nothing substantial. This was spoken to myself, me believing that the adults around me had more important considerations, and so I would keep the disappointment to myself, best I could. And why were not the others complaining. Why did not the passengers of the car rise up, pounding the walls, yelling dissatisfactions, "We cannot see the St. Lawrence River. Don't you realize this is the most powerful river in the world, even the Danube being lesser. This river is a wonder of the world! There is a reason to see this! This is a spectacular river, greater even than the Mississippi! Why are these train tracks built inland, away from the river, built by jaymen I would say, by those with no interest in nature's monuments."

When I carry on like this, I begin to believe I am a little of my father, wanting beauty more than anything else, giving no regard for the practical. I can spot it in my personality and it rises up at times like these. There is much of the poet in me. Please God, to remove it.

* * *

TORONTO IS COMING INTO VIEW, WE ARE APPROACHING IT from the east, and soon we will be into Union Station, Toronto, Canada. Upon arriving, I was thrilled with this train station, such a remarkable building. Thinking about it, perhaps because there are no ancient buildings in Canada, as a young country the citizens create instant palaces, Union Station being palatial even by European standards, featuring much granite and gold filigree, a long colonnade fronting the building, accented by double porticos. Inside is seen a huge vaulted ceiling, and a shining, vast hall. The purpose of such grandiose is perhaps to give those arriving or departing Toronto the feeling of being part of something really important.

Personally, my head was spinning.

THE TRAIN CONNECTION STARTED US DOWN TO the final leg of our journey. We arrived in Simcoe at an awkward time. This is a Sunday morning, the little red train station on Metcalfe Road is deserted with only a clerk sitting behind the ticket wicket, wearing a peaked accountant's cap, reading a dime novel, which he covered up with a train schedule upon seeing us come in. Our luggage had been placed in the centre of the platform, and we needed transportation to the farm, about six miles out of town. My father asked the clerk if there was a wagon for hire here. "No, not on Sunday mornings," he said, "most wagoneers as Anglicans are at church of a Sunday morning."

Well, there were no Anglican wagoneers around, but an Irish Catholic one showed up, allowing that he would be more than pleased to transport the family and its belongings. He, too, was a recent immigrant to Canada, but he felt out of place here, he said, in Norfolk County, since most of his kinfolk migrated to Newfoundland, or maybe Prince Edward Island, he being the only Irish "cuss" here. No lull in conversation as he offered his family's history, going back several generations, County Mayo, Roscommon, Tullamore, Bray, etc., etc., yabble yabble, and on and on, complaining about conditions here, about the poorness of the wagoneering business in a minor town of this size, the farmers giving similar services offered in the down time between the collection of crops, not required to be licensed as in Europe, letting anyone into it, including the triflers, cutting into the income of serious wagoneers such as he. Now pointing at his two huge horses, "I need to maintain Big Bart and Jenny there, and Big Bart eats a whole bale of hay a day, Jenny a half bale, taking most of the yield." Now, a thoughtful silence followed by, "Well, I didn't starve in Ireland and I'll be damned if I am going to starve here." He says this, as though starvation can simply be willed away. But that's the Irish for you, just dreamers really, set loose in a practical world, if a problem arises just dismiss the obvious outcome, and everything is okay again. But I must say, the Irish pulled a fast one on their conquerors centuries ago when forced to abandon their own tongue of Gaelic and required to speak only English, which they did and then when the Anglos were distracted, the Irish ran off with the language making it their own. Well, just look at the number of Irish writers and poets, and persons of art. Many, many are Irish; forced to change tongues, okay fine if that's what you want, but we will give you a lesson you will not soon forget. We will take your language and make it our own. Possess it. Turn it over to ourselves.

And here it went, talk, talk, talk. The driver sitting on the wagon for twenty minutes before he even told his horses to start the six mile journey, finally pursing his lips, giving a rapid kissing sound, and then touching the horses' flanks with a tap of the rawhide whip.

Perhaps I recognize the Irish behaviours because Hungarians, my stripe, are sometimes named the Irish of Central Europe, and that's just fine, we don't mind the comparison when speaking of our temperament and general outlook, but we are much better when it comes to cooking, for example the Irish boiling everything in sight, giving no regard to proper seasoning, just wolfing it down and let's get back to the Irish mist. And so my father and this Irish driver continued the exchange. Time went quite quickly as our wagon moved along, because I have always enjoyed overhearing the conversations of adults, which I was hearing plenty of right now, served up with little tiddle bits of life in Norfolk County, me looking to learn what I might expect.

Two hours are gone by now and the house comes into view. As the wagon turns in to the lane we are met with the sight of a three-story house, a grand home really, built of a beautiful yellow brick, contrasted with orange brick cornices, a turret tower in front, a widow's walk atop, and a very large lawn in front. An excellent house originally built by a United Empire Loyalist, a returning military commander. I should explain that the Loyalists were given generous land grants by the British at that time, if they chose to leave the United States in the revolution war of 1776. These were given prime land and financial assistance in the construction of a suitable house in Ontario since this would be the only remaining place of English interests in the New World. Most said they were returning through loyalty, but I am pretty sure that the offering of a handsome piece of property put some reason in it. But, goodness gracious, why to build a house with a widow's walk? Told to me later, the widow's walk was always a small observatory room with glassed walls and all, always built on the highest point of the house, the purpose for a wife to go to the top of the house and peer out to see if her missing ship's captain husband is finally sailing home, or is she now officially a widow.

The widow's walk on our new home was not a true widow's walk, at all. Think about it, why a widow's walk on the roof of a farm's house, the sea thousands of miles away? There is no sea here, no boats, or missing ships or anything aquatic. The simple answer is, this one was used to observe the farm workers out there in the fields during harvest time, answering the question, is the work getting done or are they just sitting down on their duffs.

Our Irish driver was impressed upon seeing the house, remarking saying, this is quite a home.

My father cleared his throat not once but twice, taking time to find just the right words to explain his acquirement saying, "Well, I became impressed with its design. This is not the usual house you would find in the country of my birth, the country of Hungary, and that's exactly why I chose it, fulfilling a need for something different, something of the New World. Oh, I quite enjoyed the housing back there in Hungary, of a pleasant design, but I see this house here as a new beginning, different from before." Plus saying, "the furniture in this house is just magnificent. Some of the tables, especially on the upper floor, are so large and custom made, that they had to install the furniture even before the walls were finished, just to fit the furniture in. The previous owner fell to bad times and so I was offered this house and farm at a bargain price and on very good terms, the previous owner having the mortgage foreclosed by the bank."

The previous owner would not be the first to have the mortgage on this fine property foreclosed, as it will come out later.

Offloading our goods, my father became his nervous self again. Instead of enjoying this return, he became agitated even at little things like a steamer trunk stuck, him jerking the end of it, two hands on the leather handle bouncing the trunk on the wagon floor, annoyed at just about everything. This man is not normal. He is be-jittered by the smallest of things. Even as a child I could see this. Perhaps I was given the instincts of Oma being able then as a child to analyze people problems. My siblings took everything in their stride, not even noticing the extreme state of my father.

But I saw it as a dark cloud coming up.

OUR FIRST WINTER IN CANADA BEGAN. WE children were enrolled in the district's one-room schoolhouse and once again, just like in Becse, I fell in love with my teacher. She was Miss Simpson, an American lady teaching in Canada for a different experience, and perhaps she gave us Petri children a little too much attention, out of kindness, us not speaking much English, feeling isolated from Becse.

"Notice the Petri children," she told the class. "Notice how neat they come to school. Klara, Bela, Hanna and Zarah, and properly polished their shoes are."

Those damned shoes. This is my father's influence even in the schoolhouse. Well, here is why. He made absolutely certain that we kids paid special respect to shoes. You have heard the saying 'The cobbler's child has no shoes'? Well, that means the cobbler is so busy trying to make enough money to feed his family, that he makes only shoes for others, his children having no shoes, those who should have the best, have none.

Well, that wasn't true in my father's house. We had plenty of shoes. He would work late into the night, fashioning and crafting his children's shoes out of matched leathers, meaning hides from the same animal, grains going in the same direction, shoes made perfect. But because of all this effort, woe awaits the child who does not maintain properly these crafted shoes. Waxed and shiny at all times, even on muddy days. "Notice the Petri children, class. Notice how spic and span their shoes are."

This is disgusting. I very much wanted to be noticed for more than shoes, the shoes my father made, required to be kept shiny and clean. I wanted to be known for my interest in things, in word spelling and sums, my generally high outlook to life at school. But no, always the damned shoes were brought up to the class, happening more than once.

Why not say, "Notice Zarah, this little girl here, not born in this country but wanting to know its history; why the Loyalists came back from the United States or why the word 'principal' is spelt in two different ways, 'principal, and 'principle,' why use one word two different ways, as in the English language; no one else does this, is there a shortage of words of English, or what?" And, why is there laughter from classmates when I say, "Before I go to bed at night I wash my teeth," corrected by them to say I *brush* my teeth. Are not washing and brushing the same thing? And where did the English get their language from, anyway? And who was Emily Pauline Johnson? Where did she come from? Things of that character. Not shoes. Not shiny shoes. These other things are of more importance.

* * *

IN THOSE FARAWAY DAYS IN CANADA, AT YEAR'S END, THERE would be a Christmas concert held with children singing songs and giving recitations of a Yuletide nature. In my case, there is this one-act play in which Indians give a war dance, in which I serve as an Indian maiden, being small and skinny and dark complexioned. One boy is supposed to give us a hand signal, and we all throw up our arms at once, unified, to the beat of a rhythm band. Well, the assigned signal boy gets it wrong every time. Finally Miss Simpson chooses me, the Indian maiden to give the signal, the boy fired from the job. I take the job very seriously and I get it right, giving the signal by the sound of the piano and the children's rhythm band which is made up of banging spoons against metal pie plates. In spite of the clatter I get it right, every time. I am proud of myself and pleased in the confidence shown in me by Miss Simpson, and I looked forward to Christmas Concert Night, December 19, 1924, a night that was spoilt by the actions of my father. Not to be believed. Here is what happened: On hearing there was to be a school concert, my father made it his business to attend one of the rehearsals, and then saying to Miss Simpson, that perhaps for some of the adults who would be attending the concert, perhaps he might be allowed to recite a poem, perhaps a Hungarian poem, but giving notations in English, so all could understand, so all could feel the beauty of the poem, but getting the message, too. Hard for Miss Simpson, my teacher, to say no to my father. So she okays it, my father to recite an 18th century ballad.

It is now concert night and we have all excitedly arrived at school at seven o'clock in the evening. Even being at school at a dark hour was exciting being the first time all the lights were on; we never have this in regular classes, plus there is an audience of adults sitting at our desks and we can hear the audience out there behind the curtain making the event even more exciting. The only adult back of the stage, which had been built of milk crates and strong boards, was my father. This proved embarrassing enough with the other kids asking who is this, what the heck is an adult doing back here? Well, my father was waiting to go on, that's what he was doing back there. He had committed a Hungarian poem to memory and was about to recite it, with necessary translations to English, which would have meant a third translation really, since many Hungarian poems were originally written in Latin.

And now the embarrassing part: The teacher goes on stage to say that Zarah's father, himself a poet, would now recite a poem in Hungarian, a translation offered in English at the same time, which should be a very interesting experience for all of us. There is polite applause. The audience is filled with parents many of which are farmers, some merchants, but these are small town persons with very strict rules of conduct. My father, now sitting on a tall stool which he had brought from home, a red stool, one leg forward, one arm on his waist, another arm free to move like a music conductor, giving proper emphasis on the important parts.

"I am about to recite from my memory a poem by one of the romantic poets of my country. This is a poem about love. I am not meaning the kind of love one has for his child, or such, I am speaking here of *adult* love. A young couple newly married. I am speaking of *physical* love."

The audience now squirmed in their seats, several clearing their throats, I could hear all this from back of the stage with the words "physical love" popping up from nowhere. For them, such talk is private, not for public. My father is breaking rules.

And I become humiliated. There is a shocked look on Miss Simpson's face as my father begins, she an unmarried lady, even the mole on her face turning red because this poem is about *touching*, about *touching* this, *touching* that, expressing love in a *physical* way, important as a *binding* for liaison according to the poem, and on and on.

At the end there is weak applause, only a few people for politeness reasons, and then reining themselves in, quitting the clapping, others giving no applause, at all. Luckily for me, it was the last thing on the bill, and I would be there for just a few humiliating minutes more. It was spoilt. My first Christmas Concert spoilt. Instead of a lot of enjoyment from the evening, a lot of congratulating each other on a nice presentation, all I got was this embarrassing occurrence and the other children looking at me, puzzled, wondering what this *physical* love was all about, this touching business, and why the amazing look on the faces of the audience.

And don't suppose for a moment that the sparse applause upset my father, no not at all. His belief was that this mild response to his recitation was a true sign of respect. "They were clearly astonished," he later said, "by the power of 18th century poetry."

26 SPRING CAME, AND MY FATHER DIED. IT WAS rumoured that he died by his own hand, but no one would confirm it; it was all very hush hush. Or, perhaps his death was as much from a broken heart. My father did the foolish thing of buying a farm not for the purpose of making a living, but more for the beauty of the house; a grand house of yellow brick, with a huge lawn in front. The substantial money he and my mother had accumulated working as a cutter and cook team in the forests of Wetaskiwin was now gone. Think of it. The expense of travelling back to Europe to pick up his children, of coming back to Canada again, the pledged money on a mortgage, the length of the winter in Norfolk County, and no production animals in the barn, just empty. All of this was simply too much. So, now history was in repeat, and for the second time, the bank was foreclosing the mortgage on this selfsame property. My father was losing his farm, his gorgeous house, a work of art, and his sanity leaving with it. He had no means to pay for any of this. No means of production. He had no reserves. He had no ability to begin planting spring crops. He had no horses, no cattle, not even a chicken. And do you remember the time on the train trip to Budapest when I told him Oma had gone to her sisters for money for him, and he was so shocked by that, so upset, so bedevilled? Well, now he simply would not ask for further money to save the day. Not for any reason. His help system was entirely gone.

And just generally, he was a fish out of water, as they say, and there is no place for dreamers in a practical world, there is room only for serious production, and my father was in no position to produce anything for sale.

He was a poet for goodness sakes, living with the soul of a poet present; the burdens of life out of balance with benefits.

So, he took his own life. Can you imagine the sense of terror that those who turn to suicide must have? It is against every purpose of nature. Can you imagine the final moments of my father's life, what went through his mind, the sense of failure to himself and to his family, five children and one naïve wife? His actions of course now simply made things worse. The husband and father dead, the mortgage foreclosed, all going on in this foreign country, thousands of miles away from home and village help.

We never talk of his final actions at our house. It is unmentionable. Worse, he was given a pauper's funeral, only my mother in attendance, his children kept away from a horrendous event; no Catholic burial for this suicider either, the priest remarking that my father had done a cowardly thing, why give him burial attention at all. My mother had to deal with that, too. And he is resting still in this year of 2007, in an unmarked grave in Hamilton in the province of Ontario, my mother first not having enough money to pay for a stone, later too bitter to buy one.

So, he has a small square marker with a number on it. The poet is now a number.

And, one might ask, why did the bank support him in buying the farm in the first place? I will try to make sense of that. I believe my father charmed the manager. I believe, sitting in the bank manager's office, he cleared his throat, and now eyes to the ceiling, began to recite a poem of great beauty, his handsome bass voice echoing in the room, giving a superb performance, the small town bank manager thinking: culture is here; culture has come to request financing of a home, a Loyalist's home as art, an appropriate home for a poet. And the small town manager, surely against his better judgment, pressured by the power of this unusual event, enraptured by the performance before him, submits.

That's how he got the financing.

And his suicide should be no surprise. Hungarians are very good at this, being surpassed only by the Japanese in numbers of suicides every year. But there is a serious difference; the Japanese commit to suicide as an act of honour but for Hungarians it is to protest the futility of life.

Or some say in a jokey way, it's from listening too much to Wagner.

27 I HAVE SPENT TOO MUCH TIME SPEAKING OF myself. I have not much mentioned my siblings, my Klara, my Bela, my Hanna. And there is good reason for this. As much as I loved my siblings, they are not cut from the same cloth, so as to speak. Their interests are different than mine. Closest to my personality and my interests was my sister Klara, her appetite too big for her britches, so as to speak. But she had much the same outlook as me, the same curiosities, but she kept close to our mother, and I did not. I found others more interesting than the members of my own family, probably because my family was an experience I had already covered, me going in for new things, for new people, for new events, collecting new knowledge.

Next in line, my brother Bela, given my father's name Bela, which is great in irony since Bela is not at all like my father, being more in nature like my father's father, who carried the name of Csaba, the name of Attila the Hun's eldest son. Further irony by the fact that great grandfather Csaba was very much a gentle person, while Attila the Hun was coarse and crude. Well, there you are.

And my sister Hanna, poor Hanna, always accepting things exactly as offered. Is this a good thing? Some would say yes, but I would say no. Those things seen as not proper are in need of adjustment, which cannot be done in silence. My politic attitude is socialistic if you want to know the truth of it, the care and feeding of the weakest among us. Remember the kitten I saved back in Becse, the one I found in the bag in the river, the one my Oma spirited away? Well, that kitten is symbolic of the weakest among us, for whom I give great regard. Everyone should complain of injustices especially if affecting the powerless. But for Hanna, don't rock the boat is her motto, just leave things as they are or they might get worse, that's what she thinks. And she is wrong in this matter. Shoddy deeds left unattended get shoddier, that's what I have found. Scream at social injustices when you find them. Push for alteration! Make things better here on earth, if you can! But be careful as you go about doing this, because it is important to know what in life to change, and what to keep unchanged. Not to throw the baby out with the bath water, etcetera, etcetera, etcetera.

That's what I think.

AFTER WE HAD LOST THE BEAUTIFUL FARM, AFTER my father's death, after the grieving, after chaos, we moved to 21 Peel Street in Simcoe, Ontario, the six of us now required to live in a two-bedroom flat above what is today a second hand book store. This is a big reduction from the beautiful farm house, the one of fine-looking yellow brick, with red brick cornices, turret tower and widow's walk. Now all of us are squeezed into just two rooms, all together, days filled with fear and insecurity, my mother crying into the night, the rest of us too tired to cry, covering our heads with a pillow, selfishly willing oneself to sleep, to heck with the rest. And we were penniless. Not a farthing, not a forint, not a penny, not a dime. So flat broke that my father's funeral, with just my mother and his coffin and the driver present because the Catholic priest was not willing to serve a suicide, was finally paid for by state welfare, my mother sarcastically saying, "Well, look at that now, the Nation's Poet is given a state funeral."

So bitter was my mother.

Well, you would be too. Think about it, her life was just as hard as his. And he took an early exit, not staying for the resolution, and she is stuck with it. Here she is, living above a store at 21 Peel Street with all the problems of keeping a family, even her baby Deno making a fuss, colicky with abdominal pains, the coughing of the infant making it impossible for all to sleep. And, amazing, those persons who say that troubles bring a family closer together are dead wrong, because the troubles were tearing us apart, everyone short of temper, seeking their own relief and doing so at the expense of the others.

But it is correct for me to say that the little town of Simcoe did its best for us. Word got around about this father doing himself in, his European wife and children left penniless by a mortgage foreclosure. A mortgage, I might add, that should not have been granted in the first place, my father charming the bank manager with those recitations and dramatic use of voice, reciting from memory this over-long epic poem, a classic, yes, a solid mixture of love and patriotism. Powerful stuff. And the bank manager was apparently not immune to the effects, thinking, how can I reward him.

None should offer loans on the basis of a poetry reading. In doing so, you bring damage to both lender and borrower. The proper place for poetry is for summer Sundays in the parlour. Offered up for distraction only.

The town did its best to help us. I believe Miss Simpson, my public school teacher, was at the head of the help, visiting the town's influential families, informing them of the terrible effects of my father's passing. And the influential families responded, keeping a Christian answerability. So, jobs were found for each of us, to help make a little money. I had been found a job too. And here's the irony of it all: do you remember when Oma and I went to Budapest to visit her sisters? Remember when I met their household chambermaid, a little girl of twelve? The little girl whose job it was to keep the bedrooms neat, and to take out the potty with the urine of adults, and I was so complaining that little girls should not be required to do as such? Well, the same situation came to me. My sister and brother, being older than me, were found jobs at the knitting mill in town. But too young for a factory job, I was placed with a prosperous farm family with the job of chambermaid. Exactly! The job I thought improper for a child back in Becse was handed to me here in Simcoe, picking up two dollars a week by looking after the elderly man's bedroom, changing the sheets and taking away the night potty.

A chambermaid, at the age of thirteen years, just like that child in Budapest!

There was a good part to this. I was now living with the farm family, and lucky for me, away from 21 Peel Street, all crowded, all arguing, all unhappy. A child should not want to leave her home and that should be a last thing in her mind, but I was eager to leave, this was not a normal home, the father dead by his own hand, the mother in misery, best to get out.

Now working as a chambermaid, I could no longer attend school, which was my favourite thing to do. Three years of school in Becse, one year of school in Canada, and that is my total education. Not much. Luckily, I was always good at my sums, so I could easily add and subtract as required in later adult life. In reading, my education in the English language came from the bible, the King James Version, at every opportunity, knowing that there was nothing bad in here, and much for the good. That was the total of my education, along with the public library; everyone is welcomed in there. I am self taught and I think I did a pretty good job of it, sometimes using an English word incorrectly, but all in all, a pretty good command of a language that is very difficult to learn. To this day, I rarely speak Hungarian or the German that I have, preferring the English, difficult as it might be.

The prosperous farm family would send me home on Sundays only, insisting that I get Sundays off, and so I wondered: with me away, who then took the old man's potty out? The mother-in-law? The wife? Or, and now I was giggling to myself, or did he finally get up to dump it himself?

* * *

I REMEMBER THE DATE EXACTLY, SEPTEMBER 9, 1923, we received a letter by post from Becse. Opa's heartbeat is irregular, Oma writes, and he needs a diuretic medicament made by the American Upjohn Company, not yet available in Europe. Can we obtain such and send it? He has considerable pain in the form of angina, and he is dizzy, complicating things with having only the one leg, and he can no longer work in the field, and Oma now needs to do everything. Thank God she is healthy and willing and strong and still pleased with her soul mate, ill or not, proving that she was the lucky one in this family having a true soul mate, all others, my mother's and mine later, were not. But please, she says, obtain the medicament; a written prescription is attached.

Sitting at the window, still crying now into the second year of my father's death, my mother says, "Let them live without the diuretic. I am living without a husband."

My mother made no effort to send the medicament.

 TWENTY ONE PEEL STREET REGISTERS STRONG with me. My sisters Klara and Hanna and my brother Bela were working at the knitting mill, jobs given in kindness by the owner knowing our circumstances, and the income was reasonable. The owner was very impressed with how hard Klara could work, and she informed them that she had a sister, lying about my age, and how her sister would be equally as good, and this would get me out of the chambermaid business, the job of emptying the dreaded pot. Never mind, she said, the work at the mill is clean.

So I was interviewed for the job, but the owner said how can a person so small and skinny be sixteen, which I was not, being only fourteen and small even for fourteen. She doesn't eat much, was Klara's explanation, saying I am a sometime eater only, and too fussy, staying away from gravies and meats, staying pretty well with vegetables. Her favourite sandwich is unbuttered bread and sweet cherries, or any fruit in season, which sweet cherries are now and she even eats grapes with bread. This is Klara explaining my skinniness to the knitting mill owner.

After much discussion the owner gets into a jokey mood and I am offered the job, which I am happy to accept. And he even calls me Miss Zarah out of politeness. So, at age fourteen, I am now Miss Zarah, and I liked the sound of that. I am in a factory working a ten hour day being standard at the time, before unions came along. And did I mind? No, not at all. The knitting mill was a fabulous place with huge looms, a place as big as an arena, all the mechanisms in line, being fed by bobbins. My job was to watch the bobbins, the ones with the yarns on them, to make sure they don't run out or break. If they run out or break, wow, what a problem, there will be a missing line making the fabric to look like a runny stocking, hundreds of yards of fabric would be spoiled, creating tremendous damage. So, I was given a big responsibility as a young child, and I truly wanted the responsibility. Never in my life have I run from responsibility, and you can be sure the bobbins never ran out on my watch, all knitting clear and perfect.

Back at 21 Peel Street, my mother was lonely just looking after her baby, her older children away each day in providing the income for the household; we all brought our money home to be budgeted for this or that. And that's when my mother announces that she wants to move to Hamilton, Ontario, where there is a settlement of Hungarians on Beach Road, to be among her own kind she says, not needing then to use the English language in which she was always looking for the correct word, being embarrassed in its improper use. I was often embarrassed in the use of English, the words sometimes too similar, instead of saying I would be taking a walk in the park, I would come out with a walk in the pork, the two words too similar, everyone at school laughing at my expense. Or when saying the word "observer" coming out as "absorber." So, when you hear about foreign people staying in their own district in big cities and you wonder why, just remember that there are tremendous embarrassments for the newly arrived. Everything is upside down.

One more word about 21 Peel Street before leaving it, as my mother is determined to do. I see this place as the dividing point between child and adult. This is where my childhood ended and adulthood began, 21 Peel Street is still on my mind.

30 HAMILTON IS A LARGE CITY IN CANADA, AND IT IS said to be very much like Pittsburgh in the United States, with a great number of Europeans willing to work hard and long hours in factories. Many steel plants are here, but also many knitting mills. Now my mother had four resourceful children who were very savvy in the knitting game, each experienced and each given a very good letter of recommendation from their former employer in Simcoe saying, "The Petri children are exceptional at their assigned tasks, with Zarah especially good at the bobbins, Hanna is good with carding, Klara is very good packaging and lifting being strong, and Bela is excellent at maintenance, being so first-rate with his hands." Well, goodness gracious, a letter like this is a real job getter.

In less than two weeks, we obtained work in the Mercury Mills, a producer of threads. This was a very important company built in Hamilton by Mr. Penman, famous for his boxer shorts, located on Cumberland Avenue between Prospect and Gage. An impressive building this was, with a huge thirty-foot limestone sculpture of the Roman god of commerce, Mercury, looking down at the workers coming in each day. The Romans would have been distressed to see their symbol used in such a way, but perhaps as you have read, all the factory owners of the time had huge feelings of success, having the ups, wanting to show off their business accomplishments. Mr. Ford did such with that huge hospital in Detroit that he built, as much for health as for the ups. So, that is what Mr. Penman did with that huge carving of Mercury put above the entrance of his new factory. What value is there in success if you can't brag and shake the rag, as it is said. This proves that people never really grow up, just changing from little children to big children, but this time with money, still saying, look at me Mommy, look at me, look at what I can do!

In Hamilton, we moved into a much humbler place on a street called Cheever, right in the middle of the Hungarian district, my mother comfortable now to walk to the butcher shop of a morning, being able now to request cuts of meat in her own language, bidding good morning or good evening to other sidewalk pedestrians in Hungarian, the language of her comfort. For her, living on Cheever was like living in Hungary in many ways. Finally my mother was half happy.

One terrible, unforgettable day on Cheever, I had a low down fight with my mother. Me yelling, how stupid! How ridiculous can you be! Where the hell is your brain? What are you thinking? Just of nothing! You idiot woman!

She is unmarried and had become pregnant and now, her sixteen-year old daughter is screaming at her mother that what she has done is improper, unfair. Didn't she forever chide us on the same subject? So often she said, never bring humiliation to our household with a pregnancy. And now, here she is. She is the one who has done it! Not her young daughters who kept the trust and never risked a pregnancy, kept chaste.

And now she! The mother commits the humiliation.

Thinking now, I try to find excuses for my mother's indiscretion. I cannot know what happens to a woman when her husband dies and she is left alone since such is not my experience, but I am thinking, perhaps to reassemble life, to get going again, she will accept even a wrong opportunity. And surely, this is not innocent, youthful love. This is serious adult business.

That's what happened. And it humiliated me. It humiliated Klara and Bela and Hanna, too. Grown children, their widowed mother pregnant at a time when such was not acceptable, especially when her great lover flees the coop. He leaves for Toronto to hide from his responsibility, my mother in bigger trouble than ever, more vulnerable, and I add, more teary than ever.

Nor would this be the last time.

I AM NOW SIXTEEN YEARS OLD AND IF I AM ALLOWED to say, given some of my mother's good looks, I have stopped being skinny and now merely thin, with a very good figure and all for a girl just five feet tall; smaller people usually get fat since there is so little room to put it, but I was fortunate in having an easily satisfied appetite, just a few favourite foods, and none very rich in fats. A nice red tomato, eaten in the hand like an apple, with a salt shaker at the ready, I call that a delicacy and I would often fill up on that. Well, for goodness sakes, there is nothing fattening to this at all.

Klara of course, would pack the calories in. Her lunch box to work was always filled with meaty and sweet things, she having a penchant for richer foods, saying she is preferring to enjoy the finer things in life. My other sister Hanna, was a sort of mixture of the two of us, both in personality and appearance, always weighing a little more than me, a little less than Klara. My brother Bela, always a skinny and inquisitive person, too busy to eat, inventive really, fiddling with machines, which made him an important addition to the Mercury Mills mechanical staff, with so much machinery around.

Properly now in our teens, the Petri children begin dating, never just boy and girl but in small groups, not wanting to get into pregnancy problem, leave that one to my mother.

I started dating Poor John. I call him Poor John because he was such an inadequate soul, never capable of knocking the ladies off their feet, always awkward although I cannot say he was necessarily shy and he was of reasonable good looks. It is just that Poor John is very short of dating skills. But maybe that's what appealed to me about him. He was not flashy, not that he wouldn't like to be, just that he wouldn't know how to pull if off, not able to play the part of a swain. But he was essentially an honest, if not fully dull boy, nothing exciting going on here, a date often just a walk on the green, and maybe a double dip ice cream from the vendor in LaSalle Park, and on some occasions even a ride on a jitney. Wow! Whoop de do! Gee whiz! Well, that was the very best that Poor John could come up with, but we had some other things in common.

He is an immigrant German boy, alone in a foreign country, and I, a young girl living at home, at serious odds with my mother, my mother being the sad case I have described. My mother's only interest now is to attend plate night at the local movie house, going every Wednesday, living her life through the pictures on the screen, imagining romances perhaps, giving some kind of relief to her, a housewife without a husband and another infant now, the days running long, and plate night at the movie house temporary relief, a case of see a movie, get a plate, one more time. She has more plates in her kitchen than you can imagine, stacks here and there, she saying they can be given as gifts, but no one else in the neighbourhood even wanting a gift of them, since everyone else attends plate night too, such a huge success on Wednesday night at the Delta Theatre, the manager smartly expanding it to Monday and Tuesday, causing even more plates showing up on Cheever Street. I would say an overflow.

But my mother loves those movies, describing to us the adventures of Buster Keaton and whosoever. And she gets a secret thrill from the activities of smoky ladies, the ones like Joan Crawford or Lillian Gish. These are the heavy romances, chests heaving, breath gone short, a puff on a cigarette and then a long kiss, some couples even falling over on the couch, on the screen is seen two cigarettes burning alone in the ash tray, meaning something else is going on, guess what. Her love for the films and plate night ends sadly, because just around the corner from where she lives is the Living Saints Gospel Centre, my mother visiting the place of an evening, suddenly becoming religious. This new-found faith forbids entertainment of any kind, so she struggles with the forbiddance of the movie house and sad to say, the means of spicing her dull life is now verboten, the chief deacon of Living Saints Gospel Centre gladly pocketing the weekly movie money, telling her it goes to do God's Work. Oh, sure. I heard that one before. Like God needs the ten cents.

Poor John is now my steady boyfriend, and we are not interested in the movies, we are only interested in getting our stalled lives going, so at sixteen, him at twenty-six, we decide to marry. Why not? And you might inquire, is this the kind of romance my mother might see in the movies? Or, is it the kind of marriage I imagined for myself when I was a child? Not at all. This is just a chance for life improvement. So, that is the reason that Poor John and I do the deed. There is no huge romance in the offing on this one, just a chance for mutual security, just something to build upon; we are tired of being waifs. We are married on September 24, 1927 in Hamilton, Ontario, everything going wrong on the wedding day, and I might add, in the marriage following. But no matter how chancy our marriage became over the next fifty-five years, neither of us would ever consider divorcing. We seemed to understand, without saying, that you have to take a certain amount of crap in a marriage, not as today where no one wants to take any crap at all, each accusing the other of the crap, not recognizing that crap is not a respecter of persons, just that people are hard to get along with, disagreements always to the fore, so get used to it.

I would say, of all the marriages I have known, only Oma and Opa had it in perfection. Theirs was the ideal marriage, the one humankind dreams about. Oma's marriage was poetry, the rest of us just prose.

One of the problems to our marriage was that Poor John would like to tipple. His idea of socializing would be to spend an evening with his drinking buddies. With prohibition of alcohol of any kind in Canada at that time, he would go to the speakeasies, or as they called them in Hamilton, the blind pigs, buy a mickey and drink with his buddies and finally feeling comfortable in his skin, life made more easy by bathtub gin, I am a valid human being, I have a proper place on earth, I am relevant. And I tested him, trying to find out if it was the booze or the company of boozers that he liked best. I told him I could make him very nice grappa; I have the knowledge to do that and I can brew it for him if he likes it so much. But no, his preference is to drink with his friends, perhaps to lie to each other about their accomplishments and such, their lips freed by liquor, their heads in a spin, boys changed from sparrows into eagles, fine for now, tomorrow we go to work again, what the hell, pour me another, ain't life grand?

But as dull as Poor John was he had certain talents. Well, as my Oma used to say, even a blind chicken can sometimes find a kernel of corn. As a German, he was good with machinery. A fine machinist, a shiny micrometer and slide ruler always in his shirt pocket, a visible symbol of his high achievement, him proudly working in hard steel to measurements of one thousandth of an inch for goodness sakes, on this project or that, first for the International Harvester Company, later for the Wallace Barnes Spring Making Company in Hamilton. Poor John was always good at his given tasks and always valued by his employer.

Being so good at his tasks must have sucked the personality out of him.

Could be that I might have been the cause of some of this drink. I am no sweetheart and I have definite ideas of my own and it takes someone of unusual features to deal with me.

And furthermore, I was not an enthusiastic bed companion, not wanting a pregnancy this early in the game, will this marriage work. And furthermore, the pregnancies of my mother putting the fear in me, and not forgetting Count Esterhazy either, whom I told you about earlier and how he got here, being born a bastard, the direct result of earliest condoms. So, none of these things gave confidence, only made me frightened.

But on the matter of the condoms, a great Canadian in the city of Kitchener, Ontario, at that time hearing of the low quality sheep's intestine in use, turned his attention to the use of rubber instead. Well, why not? He owned a huge rubber-goods factory in Kitchener. This would be killing two birds with one stone, first providing good quality condoms for the nation, and second, getting profits while he is at it. Oh sure, some complained that the rubber condom he made were not as good as his rubber tires, some customers saying that he should have stuck to rubber boots. Which he also manufactured.

32

WE MARRIED IN 1927 AND OUR FIRST SON WAS born in 1930. So much for rubber products. We named our firstborn Daniel, a nice enough name and the name of my husband's father, such naming to grandfathers being widely done at the time. Now, here it comes. The Great Depression you have heard about? Well, I lived it. This is when the worker is out of work, and the investor is out of luck, many investors very disappointed to where some of the previous rich were jumping out of high buildings, I remember one of them from the Connaught Hotel, jumping because all his money is gone and now he needs to go work to a real job, which apparently he wasn't willing to do. Jumping out the ninth floor like that, ending up a splash on the sidewalk, people seeing it happen wondering what's up, a crowd gathering some saying, "Oh yes, he is well known in the city, things must have gone bad."

But thinking about it, I never heard of an unemployed member of the working class jumping out of a window in disappointment, killing himself. What can the difference be?

The Depression hit the United States and Canada alike. That which happens in the United States of course happens in Canada, just two beats behind. Or as one of the Canadian Prime Ministers once said about Canada and its connection with the United States, it is like a mouse in bed with an elephant. Well, guess who is in charge under those circumstances.

John and I were affected by the Depression too, not just the investor who jumped out of the Connaught Hotel. Poor John came to be out of work. His shiny micrometer could no longer protect us. But let me speak to you about Mr. Jack Lerz, who took an interest in Poor John in that bad time. Mr. Lerz owned a major barbering shop in downtown Hamilton near the Connaught Hotel, to which the important figures of the time would come to have their haircuts. Mr. Lerz was quite successful under the circumstances, a dozen chairs busily operating at once, him getting

Source: Family Archive.

Zarah becomes Mrs. John Walters on September 24, 1927.

a rake off from each one, his shop in a stylish building, twenty-foot ceilings and black and white everywhere, black and white chequered floor, even.

And as a side business, Mr. Lerz also owned a pig farm. In those days pigs were fed slop. Kitchen scraps from some of the fanciest restaurants were picked up by pig farmers at no cost, the restauranteurs delighting in the free pick up, otherwise a disposal problem. Mr. Lerz, knowing that the restaurateurs had all this leftover kitchen scraps, learning this in cutting their hair, quickly bought a pig farm, knowing there would be pig food in abundance, I'll be glad to take it off your hands.

I don't know how John became a friend to him, and thinking about it, I could never figure out why so many people liked John, him being so dull, but they did. John always had a fresh mentor coming up, in this case, Mr. Lerz.

So as it was with John out of work, Mr. Lerz hired him to drive the pig slop pickup truck. One thing about John, he always did what needed to be done, being as they described in those days "a good provider," in this way he was reliable, never kidding himself about the necessity to work. But he had to swallow a certain amount of pride, driving the truck, stopping in at restaurants, picking up kitchen scraps in huge wash tubs, his legs buckling under the weight of such. Once working to one thousandth of an inch with expensive steels, now he is driving a pig slop truck. But interesting, still could be seen in his shirt pocket was his shiny micrometer, him keeping it up there in his shirt pocket in a leatherette pouch, symbolic of someday returning to working with expensive steels, to one thousandth of an inch, as he would say, harbouring this great responsibility, being required to choose the correct wire for a million springs, if the wrong wire is selected, all would come to a large loss in damage. Only once did he choose wrongly. An order for Studebaker, manufactures of motor cars, went wrong at John's mistake, and while John slept soundly that night, fifty machines back at the factory approved by him were turning out thousands of useless springs, later barrels and barrels scrapped. Oh my goodness! This came as the single failure in John's long career of picking the correct wires for this spring or that, nor did he forgive himself for this great error even if Wallace & Barnes eventually did so, saying what the heck John, you're going to be wrong *sometimes*.

Him saying, I must have been thinking about something else.

But as I said, it was amazing to me the number of people who actually liked Poor John, and not in an agenda way, Mr. Lerz being an example.

The rent of a house being too expensive for John and me in this time, Mr. Lerz even allowed us to move into his big house with his family: me, John, and now Danny. And when it came christening time for little Danny, Jack Lerz and his wife Bubz, no children of their own, gladly accepted the responsibility of becoming godparents. This would be in the tradition of the Lutheran Church. Well, I was a Catholic at the time, later to become a Jehovah's Witness, which was an adventure in itself, which I will tell you about later, you might be amazed.

We became close friends to Mr. Lerz, and took to calling him Uncle, even though he was almost the same age as us, but being in a more successful position. It became a lifetime relationship. Uncle Jack was a wonderful man.

At one occasion John came home and said you won't believe what happened today, me saying, of course I will believe it, just tell me, John rarely lying about anything. He said, I stopped to pick up some pig slop at a restaurant on James Street South, and backed the truck up to the kitchen in an alley. There was seen a big bunch of mixed meats, leftovers and whatnot in a tub on the platform and I started into pulling it on to the bed of the truck. An angry Chinaman came running out yelling for me to stop, I was taking away soup material. Soup material? This? All these foamy looking meats? Yes, he told me to just leave that tub alone. All he let me have was some spoiled vegetables in a hopsack. Here, you take those. John said he was sort of glad he told him to leave the stuff in the tub, saying he would have felt very bad feeding it to Jack's pigs.

Oh, he had all kinds of stories. You wouldn't want to eat in any restaurants anymore.

After two years picking up pig slop, sure enough the Depression was weakening, people began to buy hard goods again and

Wallace & Barnes came calling asking him to return to his earlier responsibilities with the micrometer and slide rule and you can be certain he was happy about that one. Uncle Jack saying sure go ahead John, there are plenty of people who can pick up pig slop in a truck, you are easily replaced.

33 I DON'T THINK I HAVE MENTIONED HOW JOHN was able to acquire all his knowledge of metallurgy. Well, this was his second time of living in North America. His parents came over to Milwaukee in the state of Wisconsin a few years before my parents came to Canada. He worked first as a broom boy at Harley Davidson, where they build motorcycles. Again, someone took a liking to John and gave him a chance to work on machines, turning out those motorcycle parts, first the crude parts, later the finer things of production. As time went on it became revealed that John had a talent for working in fine steels. Presto! Here is another fine German machinist put to work in the Harley Davidson Company. That's when he got his first shiny micrometer, the one in the leatherette case.

Meanwhile, his father starts up a musical band in Milwaukee and becomes something of a city celebrity, his band pumping out good German tunes in Milwaukee, Wisconsin, which was a German settlement in the United States at the time, his band similar to Mr. Lawrence Welk's, if you are familiar, very oom pah pah, giving out music in three-quarter time, all the time. But everyone liked it and his father was always fully booked.

A few years later his father decides to return his family to Hungary, where he buys a flour mill using all that music money. And in those days if you owned a flour mill, you owned the town, the reason being the making of baking flour from wheat was important to everyone, bread being the staff of life. These farmers had very little hard cash, so they gave every tenth bushel of wheat to the miller in exchange for grinding the other nine bushels into flour. Let's see now: if the miller gets every tenth bushel, that's like ten percent, right? Goodness gracious, I believe it is, me being good with sums. This makes the miller the receiver of ten percent of all the wheat grown in the entire region. The flour from all those tenth bushels, now owned by the miller, is sold for cash to townsfolk, those who have no wheat fields but still needing the finished flour. That is a pretty good profit. Very good, indeed.

After several successful years in Hungary with the flour mill, for reasons he never told me, John returned to North America. This time to Canada, the United States saying no to him, you had your chance, you left, no coming back again, no entrance to the United States a second time, John saying okay for you, if that's the case I'll go to Canada, which he did. That's how I came to meet him, in Hamilton, Ontario, an industrial city, a town much like Pittsburgh, with many factories presenting plenty of opportunities for John and his shiny micrometer.

On February 24, 1933, our second son was born. Again, so much for birth control methods. We named him John after John but we called him Johnnie to clearly identify him. No purpose in me standing on the back porch calling John, and both father and son come running. So, Johnnie he was. Or sometimes Johnnie-boy. On his birth Dr. Vanderburgh, who delivered him, not for money since we had none, but for two gallons of grappa distilled on the kitchen stove, freshly made and still warm. Dr. Vanderburgh said this boy will never work for a living, saying he will finesse his way making an easy path for himself which proved to be the truth of it, as you will see later.

That gave us Danny and Johnnie. Glenny, my third son, who became what they called a hippie in the sixties, later a rock and roller, wasn't here yet.

And I loved those little boys. Everything that had gone wrong in my life until that time was now corrected with those little rascals; the leaving of Becse, not seeing Oma and Opa again, the death of my father, the Depression, the sadness in seeing Poor John drive the pig slopping truck, all of this disappeared in the arrivals of little Danny, and Johnnie Boy, then later Glenn. All things were made right. And good-looking little buggers were they, handsome as the day was long. In personality, Danny was the quiet child, Johnnie was louder and bossy. Hmmmmm, I wonder where Johnnie got that outlook? Well, they always say the apple doesn't fall too far from the tree.

Which was a popular saying at the time.

34 ON JANUARY 3 IN 1938 A CHEQUE ARRIVES IN THE mail. It is from John's father, sending a large amount of money, $1,500 in a draft from the Commerzbank of Budapest, saying he wanted to help out the young couple, just to be generous. To understand the full value of this draft, with inflations considered, it would be about $65,000 in today's money. That is quite a bit.

Poor John is no longer poor.

So, like most foolish young people, first thing he buys is a new car, a 1938 Ford Phaeton, the four-door convertible model in dark maroon, with huge Coker tires and lots of shiny chrome areas. He drives it around proudly and sometimes at high speeds. At one intersection one day, he has to stop fast, and me and my Danny go flying into the front window, the glass smashing everywhere, my forehead oozing blood, the windscreen smashed, no safety glass at that time. Danny, thanks given to God, still on my lap is not hurt, but the scars from that quick stop are still on my forehead, you can see them if you look. So that's how it is; big new cash coming in leads to Sunday motoring with John, him requiring such high speeds, just foolishness, speeding out of proudness.

Even after the purchase of the impressive car there is still some money remaining, and it's my fault, I put him up to it, I wanted him to buy a farm, just a small one, a farm of cherry orchards and strawberry patches, and Damson plum trees and a Concord vineyard. Wouldn't that be nice? John nods okay. And we find one. Out in an area called Fruitland, Ontario, about ten miles from his work at Wallace & Barnes. Yet with all his spending from the Commerzbank cheque, he still has enough for a down payment if not enough for the farm in cash, and so we move to Fruitland to a nice little stucco farmhouse, orchards all around, John saying looks like the Depression is now in retreat and we'll be okay. But he was wrong about that one.

The harvest came the following year and although the crops looked good, no one was buying. Usually E. D. Smith, the canning factory, would buy the crops, but they would contract the established farmers first, the new ones needing to wait in line and John was a new one. It was a long line so John just waited. Well, you can only wait so long and then the fruit falls to the ground. That's where 1939's crop went. And we went broke again. At one point, with no fruit sales, and the mortgage still needing to be paid, I went and got a job again at a knitting mill, saving the jitney fare by thumbing for a ride, until one man picking me up, puts his hand on my knee, him asking if I want to have some fun. I was quick in my thinking to put him off by saying gee, no thanks, I'm six months pregnant and have no interest in the subject. When he stopped the car at a corner, I just stepped out of it, and started walking terrified toward Fruitland in the dark, hoping he would not follow. I walked scared stiff about twelve miles in the dark and when I got home really late, John was fit to be tied, screaming at me, where the hell have you been, me yelling back, where the hell do you think I have been?

I never gave him the awful details of that night, and he never again asked, him perhaps thinking my evening was not a good one, anyway.

And then I did become pregnant once again, resultant to family planning products, with my third child, born a boy, Glenn, the one I earlier mentioned, the one who became a hippie in the sixties. So, now it's three boys. Poor John is poor in money matters, but rich in sons. Numbering three.

Which just complicated things more. Remember how my father's farm was seized for mortgage foreclosure back there in Simcoe? Here comes the bad news: same thing was about to happen to me. Due to the bad circumstances, John and I had not made a mortgage payment for three months. We could not pay. It was heartbreaking when one day, the county sheriff arriving at our stucco farmhouse, and after reading a statement to me, with the help of two sheriff employees, started to remove our furnishings, our "chattels" as he said it, on to the front lawn and then to padlock the doors, not even requesting from me the keys. Padlocked front doors was a common sight during the Depression in Canada. To see furniture on the front lawn, padlock on the door, you would know that another family has gone broke with all the powerful consequences from that. People driving by would slow down, rubbernecking everything on the lawn, just as they rubberneck accidents today on the highway. Them thinking, better them than me.

So when John came home that evening, here am I on the lawn with all the furniture, a young mother with her three children, adjusting the baby's crib beneath a tree to avoid the sun, the infant Glenn asleep not knowing what was going on, the other two kids running around thinking this was great sport, proving once again that in ignorance there is bliss.

No place to sleep that night. I began to think, my God I am beginning to repeat my mother's life, with a husband who cannot keep his family. This is what caused my poet father to do himself in. But I need not worry about John taking his life over this tragedy, that being a Hungarian or perhaps a Japanese outcome or sometimes even a Swede but not a German, except Hitler did, but that was a special condition.

Next day was a Saturday. They always evicted on a Friday, knowing that the weekend the husband would be home to arrange for moving the chattels from the front lawn, eviction on a weekday might mean a job loss, and the bank, bless their hearts after throwing you out, would not want your husband to lose his job, too. So humanitarian. So thoughtful!

John drove his Ford Phaeton to Uncle Jack's farm and came back with the pig slop truck to move our things to another house he found in the area, a rental from a man who did not expect payment in advance, just pay me when you can. He was a Mennonite. John worked all Saturday and Sunday, the truck being able only to take one or two pieces of furniture at a time, coughing and complaining, even doing a back fire, John squeezing his eyes shut at the sound of it, the truck making much noise while carrying our worldly goods to the next house, the rental.

These troubles were not good for our marriage. As I told you, our marriage was not a big romantic thing. This was not a marriage of romance but just a way to improve things. We were two lonely people in a strange land, and that's where our marriage came from. Not violins in the moonlight or a single rose in a Waterford bud glass, or a glass of champagne held high to toast a wondrous thing.

Just travel through life beside me, and be my friend.

Our marriage was just practical. I thought it would be good enough, in other words serviceable. But even the practical reasons were going out of it now. John took to drink, the easy relief. I took to religion. I became a Jehovah's Witness. I was a weak Catholic, not ever believing in the power of the priests, wishing a more ordinary belief, and I found it in the Jehovah's Witnesses where there was no priest, no minister, just laymen speaking of what I thought was beautiful truth. Even those who had no talent for public speaking, the awkward among us, the self conscious, the stammerers, were allowed to stand up in front of our gathering, and express their love for Jesus Christ, who I really believed was one of us, Christ having had his share of evictions too, with that no room at the inn business going on, even at his birth for goodness sakes, that was a big one.

And I thought, Oma would have loved this religion. Oma, who long ago made complaint of the old line religions, how the church was the most expensive building in Becse, built on the sweat of the poor she would say, and the priest, turning his back to the congregation through the Mass, placing himself before God, the rest of us behind him, him muttering in a bored way for the one thousandth time, his original interest long ago lost, the mass in the Latin language, everyone in the audience shut out from this important matter, just to watch, looking up.

Sheep look up.

Oma would not look up.

She would have loved the idea as do the Jehovah's Witnesses, that heaven could be here on earth if only mankind properly tried, and there is no hell, no burning place, no place of eternal damnation, that every man is fragile, so fragile that you would wonder how anyone could be cruel to any other. All suffer. No one is free of this. And you would think then, all should be sympathetic instead the common meanness seen everywhere. This would have appealed to Oma.

And I went door to door spreading the message. Comedians make sport of this. On television they always come up with jokes about this; about the Jehovah's Witnesses knocking on the door one householder saying, Great, next time bring a pizza. Do you think it is easy for us to do this? To go door to door, always unwelcome? Once I even had a dog sicced on me. 'Sic 'em,' said the homeowner. Disrespectful. He would not have understood how much courage I needed to gather, to go knocking on his door trying to bring him the Good News. And I get in return, sic 'em, me a small boned woman, not much more than a hundred pounds, and this big ignorant man with, sic 'em, sic 'em.

Little did he know that I understand animals, and I said to the dog, there King, take it easy King, and the dog slowed down, halted his growling, and then turned around to walk away. The man was stunned. His killer dog was taken off balance by a little woman, me, who with a kindly voice, told him, take it easy King, and the dog became civil.

So perhaps you can see it is never easy to knock on the door of strangers, knowing that you are despised in doing the work of Jesus Christ over two thousand years later, his influence still strong, still available and still important. But we do it. No pay.

Even John makes game of me.

But let's not listen to John about this. John is a non-believer. Albert Einstein, safe to say smarter than John, said, "It is very foolish to believe in the existence of God, but even more foolish to not believe." So, the smartest man who ever lived figures there must be something true about the God stuff. Think about that one.

But even my newly found faith gave me only moments of relief from a life that was getting away from me. In this rented house with its small rooms, I was beginning to realize how powerless I have been. I planned none of this life. I did not plan for a dour husband, mortgage foreclosures, three babies. None of this did I plan. Life just got away from me. I would now daydream, doing my household chores, sleepwalking, my mind wandering back to my childhood, the warm summer mornings in Becse, with the smell of new mown hay heavy in the air, the plum boy, me running to the market ahead of Oma, my life with Oma and Opa in that perfect place. What happened? What the hell happened! Here I am alone in this rented house except for the children, no adult here, and amazing, I am not even able to weep anymore, everything dried up, only the pain remaining, coming out as dry tears. And I thought again, my God! I *am* living my mother's life, evidence is the dour husband and the foreclosed mortgages and the many babies. Her life, exactly! Not mine. None of this was my intention. My plan would have been for a small plot of land a stone's throw from the river Tisza, and always near to Oma and Opa, perhaps me and the plum boy growing our own foods, a gentle cow perhaps, a Jersey cow, the English kind with the big soulful eyes, producing all that rich milk, much cream to the top of the bottle and fresh butter and cream the result of it. And a few fruit trees. And we would be left alone to create our life in a natural state, not as now, driving around in a stupid maroon Ford Phaeton at high speeds, proudly saying look what I got, and then losing everything, the farm turning into a rented house, the Ford Phaeton becoming a pig slop truck.

None of this should have been for me. I am a natural person, not appreciating the city or cars or the shiny things of a shiny life. I am never a jaybird filling her nest with shiny objects. I can spend an hour more amazed by the activity of a single beetle trying to move a piece of cow dung than all the modern wonders of man, everything he touches becoming condemned, green scum floating on Lake Ontario, just a few miles from here fish rotting on the beach, I walked on the shore just yesterday and death was all around me.

On the six o'clock news, they said there is now tons of garbage floating in space. There is garbage on the moon!

 I WILL CATCH YOU UP ON MY SIBLINGS BY the year 1938.
Life goes on.

Klara, the sister who rubs sandwiches on sores, has married Joseph Kardas and has two children, a girl and a boy, gets a divorce, her husband ends up in Chicago with a red haired woman; Klara's children come to despise her, not to see her ever again, a huge loss for Klara who has always been a caring mother. Later she marries a second time, the man is mentally unbalanced, put in a mental institution where he stays the remainder of his life. She gets a second divorce marrying still a third gentleman and has another child, a gift from God surely, to replace her earlier children now gone forever. She hits the jackpot with her third husband who is indeed a fine person and suitable for Klara who then loses the jackpot when he dies early from cancer, and she is alone once more.

And then there is my brother Bela, generous as the day is long, marries a woman twice his intellect, who, although she is good in the smarts department is void in the health department, eventually becoming confined to a wheelchair, and for the next forty years Bela tends to her every need and her needs are many. You can be amazed at his dedication and not once does he complain of his responsibilities, just keeping on. They have just one child, a girl who is the prize, with a good demeanour and she becomes a university professor, so parents are rewarded.

My quiet sister Hanna marries a steelworker. This is a man's man. Not a romantic, but a steelworker who is so proud of his manhood he delights in risking his life everyday in the steel mills of Hamilton, Ontario, handling molten steel rods, the job so tough it is a half hour on, a half hour off, or die from the heat and Ferenc, that's his name, thinks it's great. For him, danger is an inspiration. Those hot metal rods flying around, deadly at any moment, ready to kill, him being quick on his feet, staying alive for forty-one years of chasing molten metal rods and not once, he would say, not once did get a serious burn to the bone like some. His luck is enhanced by a teakwood carved statue of a black elephant that sits on the Philco, he pats its head before he leaves for his dangerous job each day, saying the elephant, head rubbed, keeps him from danger, and that's why after forty-one years of chasing molten metal rods he is still alive. It's the elephant responsible for the good luck.

Hanna, his wife, has the nature to always accept things as they are. No troubles at the brick bungalow on Beach Boulevard, everything fine as long as the steel mill is hot. They have two children, the boy much as his father, the daughter much as Hanna.

Here are the rest of my siblings, those arriving after the death of my father, victorious against family planning methods.

Magdi.

Joska.

Magdi is the most generous human being you can find. She opened her house to anyone in need. Her husband is the world's handsomest man.

Joska is a tinkerer somewhat like Bela, and ham radioing his interest. He built a ham radio station and installed this in his attic, broadcasting around the world, him saying gee, I talked to Africa today.

* * *

NOW WORLD'S WAR TWO IS COMING UP. I AM WORRIED SICK for my Oma and Opa. They are really getting old now, and the war is again on the horizon. How many times must they go through this war nonsense?

This time it's Communists. And I am now to wonder, did the Communists take Oma and Opa's land from them? Are they now landless? Houseless? Perhaps this is the political outcome. But I cannot imagine my Oma without her small farm, her little bit of paradise, perhaps removed from her now by the Communists.

Everyday, for at least a few minutes they are in my thoughts. They are a big piece of my life, broken off.

36 JOHN WAS NEVER MUCH OF A RENTER, SO HE WAS not pleased sending out rental cheques every month. He sold the Ford Phaeton, trading for something cheaper, and took the difference along with some casual money and got enough together for a down payment on a nice yellow clapboard house at 45 Ivon Avenue in the Normanhurst district of Hamilton, closer to his work. It was a nice little house and big enough for the five of us, and things were pretty calm.

And then the World's Second War began. That's when I went nuts. Because clearly I never forgot the dire effects of when the First World's War came to Becse, when Oma and her grandchildren, us, had to hide beneath the bed as the bullets banged into our home. On that day, the threat of death was everywhere, my Oma, she who was never frightened of anything, now shaking like a leaf, hanging onto her grandchildren, huddled beneath the bed while the big boy soldiers shoot at unarmed villagers, forgive my saying, these soldiers just no good bastards and sons of bitches; this is a proper estimation. Well, look what they did to me! To this day I remain frightened at the simple sight of soldiers even when viewed in newsreels. These are dangerous people, just young boys, now girls too, from homes where kindness was once considered, taken now to boot camps and taught to kill others of their own species, shooting with guns and how best to blow up others. It goes against nature. To this day, in my mind's eye I can see those soldiers in Becse. True, I cannot see them direct, they are at the peripheral of my vision, off to each side of my sight, but when I concentrate I can see them clearly and then in a scary way they disappear, returning when I least expect it. Here I am, squeezing my eyes shut, trying to remove the soldiers, wishing them away, but they remain, beating Opa over the head with a riding crop, him standing there holding his hands atop his head, trying to protect himself, his chin in his chest, my protector as a child looking like a schoolboy, being beaten. This happened many years ago but sometimes it makes me shake. I will never understand any of this, not if I live to be one hundred.

Can you see? Can you see how war affects children? How it alters their sense of security for the rest of their lives. And still it goes on. It goes on around the world. At any given time, I have read it, there are at least twenty-one wars going on, the children having their sense of security removed by the big boys with guns, having fun, getting adventure. You would think that every war would end immediately with the death of the first child, the soldiers looking at the dead child, becoming ashamed of their bravo actions, seeing their cowardice for what it really is. But no, not at all, here the dead child is viewed callously, the soldiers thinking, hell, it isn't my kid, it's a kid from the other's side.

Tell me, what is the suitability of that?

Always, more civilians and children die in wars than soldiers do, being a civilian is a more dangerous job than being a soldier. Compared by the numbers of civilians killed, being a soldier is pretty safe stuff.

So, as I mentioned, another war is on and again the conditions are showing up. Now in Hamilton, Ontario, preparations for attack by German diving bombers is underway. To train the public, there are practice air raid sirens being sounded at all hours of the day and night. Even cars have their headlights dimmed by putting a template inside the glass letting only a small slit of light through, keeping the moving cars from being seen from the air, keeping the city dark in the event of German diving bombers, the threat is real. These air raid practices took place on a regular basis in Hamilton, as they did in Europe, bringing back all my fears.

So I scream to John, "I will not stay here. I will not go through another war of bullets banging on the house, me and the kids beneath the bed, living Oma's life, while the big boys are shooting bombs and bullets, I will not do it." Like usually, when I become elevated, John spins his forefinger around his ear to me, indicating insanity.

And he yells back just as loud, "Well, there is nothing that can be done. We will be under attack. They are under attack even in London, England, and we will be under attack again, here. This is a world's war. Everyone is involved."

"Not for me John, not for me. Move us out of here. Sell this house. Buy a place away out in the country where the enemy has no purpose in bombing, not even to a village will I move, but to the country, open fields, no one around. That's the ticket."

I bothered him with this for months, every chance, every opportunity. Finally, he gives in to the constant pressure and I somehow believe I got him scared too, although he had never lived through a bombing circumstance as I had. But I was vivid in my argument and detailed, giving much credence to my fears. And he submits.

We found another farm, far from the city, and this was a beauty. This was one hundred and twenty acres of the most beautiful land in the Niagara region. Rolling hills were there, and meadows all green, going back a full mile from country road in the front to country road in the back. It was the old Bater farm just above the Niagara Escarpment. James Bater was the original owner, and you guessed it, he was a United Empire Loyalist too, the farm much as the one back in Simcoe. It seems wherever I go there are United Empire Loyalist considerations, this one too. Although this house wasn't nearly as splendid as the Simcoe house, but still pretty nice; yellow clapboard with white trim, two story in design, and really very pleasant.

Only one problem. There were tenants in it. The previous owner had rented it and did not require the tenants to move out upon the sale to us, allowing the tenants to stay in there. It was a surprise to us, our chattels in a moving truck, pulling up to the house and the renters still in there, the husband coming out, telling us his wife will not move, she is staying in there, he says, nothing can be done about it, that's just the way it is.

"Just a darned minute, mister, we have purchased this farm, the paperwork has been done, it has become our property and you say you are staying here, nothing can be done?"

Now, the husband renter puts his finger to his lips, ordering caution in our voices. "Keep it down. Keep it down, or my wife will hear it, bringing on terrible troubles."

"Terrible troubles, how?"

Now it really gets secret, whispering he says, "My wife is capable of placing curses. She has done this several times in her life, bringing a bad result to her foe. Please don't create a circumstance where she will do this again. I see you have three young children here. This is where she does her biggest damage, and I wish not to see this happen. I have watched the suffering to her rivals before, and I don't want to be required to witness such again. Especially, to children as you have here. So please leave. Turn your truck around and go back to where you came from, and avoid the result of my wife's curse."

And then I say to John, "These must be Romanians. Only Romanians send out curses like this. But they are sham curses. They have no currency. These are the Romanians who work the carnivals and circuses of the world, just to buffalo the population, faking supernatural powers, scaring most people stiff. Not for me."

I tell our moving truck man to remove all our furniture and place them in the front yard, this I said to prove to the renters that we are serious about staying, to prove that curses amount to nothing where experienced Hungarians are concerned. We Hungarians left all the curses behind in Transylvania centuries ago.

"Out! Out! Out of this house," I am yelling, "What kind of people are these trying to threaten my young ones with such miserable talk."

John and I and the kids spend the night sleeping on the spacious lawn in front of the house. It's a beautiful night anyway. It had been years since I spent the night outside as I had many times as a child, and now again I was on my back with my eyes to the sky, enjoying the sight of blinking stars and the wonders of the night sky, even if under such stretched circumstances. And I am in lying here, eyes skyward in amazement, having learned from Miss Lengyel, my school's teacher in Becse, that the distance in the sky is so vast that the very light that I see now is already four years old although just now getting to my sight. And it will always be strange to me that just a handful of stardust weighs tons, but floats up there, wafting around the universe in a feathery state.

These are the wonders that life gives us. Even with the troubles there are these things of amazement.

The house remains dark and silent with a single candle burning in an upstairs window. The Romanians are trying to put an additional scare on us.

Early in the morning a truck arrives and backs up to the house. The renters are in retreat. They are beginning to move their things out of the house.

I watched them, feeling sad for them too. These people were now just as homeless as John and I were back in Fruitland when the farm was whisked from under us, the sheriff reading the eviction notice to me while John is at work, his men putting our chattels out on the front lawn. So, I know the circumstance, and seeing this sight brought me serious discomfort. Still, there was no alternative but to challenge the curse, which incidentally never came to harm us.

A Romanian curse comes to nothing but a limp biscuit, as my Oma used to say.

37

COMES INTO OUR LIVES NOW, THE WARTIME Prices and Trade Board. If you don't know what this is, here is the information on it. During the Second World War, the government puts a freeze on all prices in order to control inflation because of military production affecting prices. Well, these controls are okay for city people, but for farmers it was a real problem because the prices of feed for animals go up and down with how good the growing season is. A good growing season, the prices go down because of ample supplies of food for animals, this proves profitable. In years where there is little rain, the food supplies are reduced and the prices go up, this is not profitable. That's just the way it is. Meanwhile the farmers during the war are required by law to sell their animals to meat packing houses at a government pre-fixed price, giving no consideration to what growing of pork or beef cost. The government is not thoughtful of this in pre-fixing prices, not taking the year's weather into consideration, making one to think that perhaps all government ideas start during cocktail parties where small talk is required, and then under the influence of various wines and spirits the small talk blossoms and is soon taken seriously with, sure, we will start doing that tomorrow. Sounds like a good idea. Shall I freshen up your drink?

What else could it be?

During the prices and wages freezing, John is still working on war production at Wallace & Barnes, working a lot of overtime but even this is not enough to cover the costs of the farm, which were very high. Things do not look good. What to do? It was looking like we were headed for financial disaster again, maybe to lose this farm too, this time due to Wartime Prices and Trade Board, circumstances not of our making. No! Not again! We will not allow this to happen all over again, the sheriff coming, showing his credentials, and then reading from an official looking sheet of paper the news that the mortgage has been foreclosed and the law makes possible an eviction here. And then, his two assistants starting to move the chattels out, even the drawers emptied into cartons, everything all mixed up, and all items placed on the front lawn, while the defenceless woman, her husband away to work, cries silently on the front steps, her children at her side.

Well, I will not allow this to happen again.

I told John we need to increase the income to cover this. Looks like the black market is our only alternative to going bankrupt. I am thinking we need to get into selling our farm products *directly* at prices people are willing to pay. And so I am telling him: I bet you could sell a lot of pork to your fellow workers in Hamilton, those Italians and Portuguese people really go for pork in a big way, and he says, yes he could sell a lot of pork, but that would be against the law since all is rationed.

So, I said to John, to give him confidence in the idea, I said I just checked with the Ten Commandments, which have always been my guide for proper living and there isn't one word in there about not selling meat to the Italians and Portuguese (Exodus 20: 1–17 and Deuteronomy 5: 6–21). John says sure, this is not a sin as outlined in the Ten Commandments, but he completes to say, if he gets caught with a black market pig in his car, all butchered and cleaned, he could end up in jail. I said to him, take your choice John, jail or bankrupt again, and you are not getting any younger.

You guessed it. That was when John started selling pork through black market efforts. Business thrived. Those Italians and Portuguese were delighted, buying great amounts of black market pork, John leaving for work at Wallace & Barnes most mornings with a butchered pig in the back seat, breaking the Prices and Wage Control laws every morning after his breakfast. This was his routine: two eggs and ham, pepper potatoes, pumpernickel toasted, chicory coffee, and then go break the law.

And he was always nervous about this to where his smoking cigarettes headed on the increase. He would drive those twenty miles, shudder at the very sight of any approaching police car, enter the Wallace & Barnes parking lot, approached by another car with either an Italian or a Portuguese in it, him opening the trunk and then putting the pork in. This activity at least twice a week really got on his nerves. He felt like a criminal. I told him to stop feeling in that way, he was serving a thankful public. Just to share the responsibility, on several occasions I made the deliveries, giving John a chance to get back his breath. Showing the difference in our personalities, I found the pressure inspiring.

So the day was saved by the Italians and Portuguese, them liking pork so much enabled us to pay the mortgage each month and buy additional farm equipment too, increasing production and helping the war effort in that way. Oh yes, I would say that our actions were doing much good for the government by stretching these laws, breaking them actually, passing on to them all this increased production.

There were other means by which I stretched the laws. For a good example, there was the matter of medicaments. In Europe it is the custom to produce a small amount of grappa or fruit brandy for winter consumption, for relief against winter colds, and sometimes just for celebration, a little tipple now and again, grappa as my Oma called it. But grappa is considered an alcoholic beverage by the liquor authorities in this country, and illegal to make, Europeans forbidden to make alcoholic products even for personal use as they did in Europe at that time. Might be different now. I don't know. So again I turn to the Ten Commandments, and no mention in there of grappa. Nowhere is seen: Thou shall not make grappa.

So I said to John, I will do as I did when we were first married, when I was required to leave my job at the Mercury Mills, and needing to make some money, I started into making grappa,

This is my grappa distiller made
from ordinary kitchen utensils, being
just a six gallons laundry pot and
a Chinese Wok. A few bricks, and
there you have it.

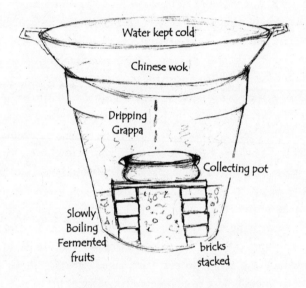

Drawing of a home distillery. Credit: Alyssa Coppolino.

selling quantities to willing customers. John says, well you know
that's against the law in this country, unlike in Europe where you
can make all the grappa you want, but you are correct in saying
this product is required for the fight against colds during the flu
and cold season. So, what's coming up next?

Well, he should have known, grappa was coming up next.
I will even tell you how to make it, but just remember it is illegal to
make and you could be prosecuted. Here's how: I use only kitchen
utensils, the reason being these utensils are not easily identified as

a grappa distiller by the Royal Canadian Mounted Police, if they break down your door looking for a grappa distiller, being illegal equipment and used for evidence against you. Not able to find a recognizable distiller, no evidence, see? So, there is no distiller as used by the Seagram Company, these are pots and pans, ordinary in nature, and to the untrained eye having nothing to do with alcohol production. I would say to the officers in such an event: goodness gracious no, you officers can plainly see these are just kitchen materials, nothing serious. Also, while making the grappa, it is a good idea to burn a little sugar on the stove top to cover the scent of grappa being cooked, which is highly identifiable to the RCMP who are educated in this, so the burning of sugar changes the odour of grappa cooking in the kitchen, to smell like buns and pound cake baking. But I would warn you: just a little sugar on the stove, not put too much, because that could enflame, firing up the grappa which is quite powerful in character, causing a blowment, flames to the ceiling burning the kitchen down, the fire marshals arriving now looking for the reason of the fire, finding pots of grappa, all of it illegal, just more problems to deal with, you wondering why did I ever get started with this in the first place, this being more trouble than the worth of it.

So, be careful. I will tell you how to do it, but you are on your own with this.

First, you use a half bushel of old fruit gone bad for each cooking, any kind will do, pears, apples, plums, the more ripe and squishy the better. Now smash these up, putting all into a large pot along with two or three cups of sugar and cover all with cheesecloth. Left for a week like this, there will be a foamy appearance atop and a strong odour of musky fruit turning to alcohol. Take a deep breath of this several times since this is a lovely odour and will keep your interest up. This is now called mash. Next is to make a grappa distiller out of common kitchen utensils in this manner.

The heat raises the temperature of the mash until it steams, the steam rising in the pot until it hits the cold water pan on top, turns to a liquid and then falls into the collection pan below. Much like cooking rice, you can check on the cooking but try to avoid steam loss. Later taking the liquid grappa out, letting it cool and then maybe colouring it a bit with some burnt sugar, giving it a nice tan tone.

But while doing this, just remember making grappa is illegal and you could go Kingston, so perhaps you would rather not. But remember, making this liquid was a requirement in Becse in Hungary, for winter cold cures. Well the reason is obvious: no drug store in business on the corner. In the old country you needed to make your own.

As long as we are talking about unlawful things, there was third unlawful thing that I did. That was the making of *mákos rétes*. What is that you are beginning to wonder, what law is this woman about to bend by going again to the Ten Commandments to get an O.K.? Well, *mákos rétes* is what some call strudel, but this Hungarian one requires poppy seeds. Well, the growing of poppy seeds is illegal in this country too, because it is used in the making of heroin, which I would never make, but everyone was forbidden to grow the poppies anyway in case there was a tendency to make it. I would say to John how foolish it is being forbidden to grow poppies just because some people make heroin of it, although we would not, John saying well that's just the way it is. And I say to John, I think I will grow some poppies, John being dead set against it, him believing he was lucky enough getting away with the black market pork sales without tempting the gods of fate with even more illegal activity, the RCMP gumshoes coming around, finding what's up.

And then sure enough, using it again for moral assistance, I go to Exodus 20:1–17 and Deuteronomy 5:6–21, the Ten Commandments being God's idea on what to do and what not to do, and as you would know, there is nothing in there about not growing poppies. I will say, poppy seeds are a very popular item with central Europeans of every stripe, so I tell John, gee, when you make those pork deliveries, maybe you can sell some poppy seeds too, increasing the income, just ask the husband if the wife would like poppy seeds for sweet goods. John saying he can do as such, since he is already illegal, and so he even sold some to a big ethnic bakery needing large amounts, the illegal strudels for sale out of sight, in the back room, and much appreciated. Along with the pork sales, the poppy seeds moved pretty quickly, John coming home with pockets full of dollar bills, emptying his pockets on the kitchen table, the table looking like a harvest. We are in the money and it is plentiful.

To grow the seeds and to keep them secret I planted the poppies in the cornfield, every second row poppies, the corn growing higher than the poppies, keeping them from sight of the RCMP while driving by, John saying you know you are foolish, the RCMP can fly over the fields by aircraft, and see the colourful poppies from the air, finding where they are and later travelling by car to your field, arresting you for illegal poppy growth.

But that's just John, he is still nervous with the black market pork sales being so successful, the Italians and Portuguese puffing up his cash flows, always asking for more, him leaving every morning with another pig, payday every day, making him very elevated, that's why the big story about the RCMP flying over my poppy field resulting in my arrest perhaps shutting down his pork business, that's what he is trying to protect.

I said, John you have incorrect information. Now I begin to giggle, later making him laugh too as I point to a calendar on the wall, the RCMP musical ride proudly displayed on the cover of a State Farm Insurance calendar, and I tell him the RCMP cannot fly over my cornfield and see the poppies, the RCMP does not have an airplane, and then I point to the calendar saying as proof,

"You can plainly see on the calendar John, they are still using horses! We're safe, John. They will never spot the poppies. They don't fly. They use horses! We will be able to see them coming!"

Now, he starts to laugh, John, with the heh, heh, heh, in low tones at first getting me started too, and I laugh in high tones, high pitched, me laughing makes him laugh now even louder, making me to laugh even higher, me needing now to sit down now, him already sitting and now slapping his knees in laughter, and then in my mind's eye I begin to believe he is laughing so much that he is going to pee himself, and then seeing this in my mind's eye makes me laugh even more and it's like an insane asylum in here; the crazy idea that the RCMP only patrols on horses, no airplanes to see the poppies from the air. And then, trying to take control, John furrows his brow trying to be serious and he says, "You watch out. They are going to come and find your poppies growing beside the corn, they will sneak up on you so you won't know they are coming and then they will arrest you for illegal growth of poppies." Now, him looking so serious strikes me as extra funny, and I begin to scream in laughter telling him, "No, no John, you are wrong, they cannot sneak up because they are highly identified in wearing—" and now I am pointing at the calendar picture again, "highly identified by wearing those bright red jackets! More than just the horses, they have on those red jackets too! Red is easy to see!"

Now he starts laughing anew, and I do too, for about ten minutes until it starts to die down, and then I point to the calendar again saying we will be able to identify the RCMP coming to arrest me, by the horses and the red jackets but also by the highly identifiable big brown pointy hats too, and that puts all the laughing into high gear again.

We are worn out with laughter, coming to a conclusion.

But it felt so good, it had been so long since we had laughed like that, all the troubles, the mortgage foreclosures, the nervousness of running a black market of pork to Italians and Portuguese, these things had weighted heavily on us, and laughter was something missing from our lives; now laughing at the RCMP picture, I began to feel the good effects of that laughter, now feeling like a kid again, although forced to live and work in an adult world. Later John actually admitted to me that on that occasion he actually peed himself. So now, whenever things got tough, and tension came to our household, I would point at the RCMP musical ride picture, the horses and red jackets, and we would start to laugh again, bringing back some of those good feelings.

So, that's how I grew my poppies. One row of corn, one row of poppies, not a single RCMP in sight. All the poppy seeds harvested in the fall, the ends of the pods cut off with a razor blade, the seeds shaken into glass jars, on sale to ethnic bakeries for the making of *mákos rétes* which I will provide you the recipe right now.

1 pound of freshly ground poppy seeds
½ cup of sugar
Grated rind of ½ lemon
½ cup of milk
⅓ cup of raisins or 2 apples chopped
2 tablespoons of melted butter

Cook the poppy seeds, sugar, grated lemon rind, and milk in a double boiler until slightly thickened. Add the raisins or apples; mix and cool it. Spread it on the strudel dough, which you can buy at the stores now and usually of good quality, which you must brush with the butter. Roll up using care to keep the filling from falling out. Now cut the roll into lengths to fit a buttered pan, and bake in a hot oven at about 450 degrees Fahrenheit for about thirty minutes or until crisp and brown. This will make ten to twelve servings.

And if you want to grow your own poppies, doing so has now

become legal. Correct, it is no longer illegal. Now you can grow all the poppies you want, not against the law. One year something is illegal, the next year not, proving that rules are not reliable. I would say it is better to open up the Good Book to Exodus 20:1–17 and Deuteronomy 5:6–21 and go ahead and do what's best for your family, and to heck with the rules.

I HAVE MENTIONED OFTEN THE JOY OF HAVING a farm. Indeed, many persons who live and work in the city say they would like to have a farm too, nature all around, the sound of the rooster early in the summer morning telling the hen to get up and get those eggs going, and fresh herbs for cooking, and most especially the interest in the animals of the barn's yard. The enjoyment of such, even the cows greeting you in the morning, giving a moo and if they could smile, you can be certain they would, but of course they can't, their facial muscles cannot go sideways. Horses even, kicking the side of their stall in the morning when you come in almost saying where the hell you been all night, how's about getting breakfast started. All the animals of the barn's yard actually react to your presence in the morning, an experience city people never get, them greeting you like an old friend, they are alive, and they know they are alive and capable of a personal relationship just as it is with people.

Sometimes I think animals are just people of a different kind.

Which we abuse. Even the cattle, we have bred them for milk production, their udders made too big, doubled, an unnatural size. Well the truth of it, cows were not intended to be producers of milk for the public, their udders so big now they almost step on their pipes when they walk, the pipes almost to the floor, even causing them to *look* foolish, which my Oma called a removal of dignity. Are there any animals in the wild with udders down to the grass? I don't think so. And yes, animals have a dignity too which should never be removed.

So, animals are manipulated for advantage. Even I did some of this of which I am not proud, which was this: one year there was more money in selling ducks than chickens, making me think about getting into the duck business. To start I buy a bunch of duck eggs to hatch for duck sales but not having a mother duck on hand, I put the duck eggs under a mother chicken, finding her in a brooding mood. To explain, during this brooding mood in poultry, the body temperature of the hen goes up, she loses her bum's feathers, exposing bare skin to put over the eggs, increasing the temperature of the eggs and hatching them in twenty-one days. Every adult hen gets into a brooding mood during its cycle. So, I thought, if the brooding hen isn't smart enough to identify duck eggs, what the heck, I'll put the duck eggs under her and give her the job of hatching ducks instead of chickens, ducks bringing a better price, the fancy restaurants sautéing duck in a fancy manner, our special is Duck a l'Orange today, Mrs. Smit. Do have some.

So I plotted against the hen. I put duck eggs under her. She accepted them although they are little larger than chicken eggs, and she started sitting on them. Trouble is, I didn't know that the hatch cycle for ducks is about ten days longer than the cycle for chickens. When she is sitting, the hen will leave her nest to feed and drink water only once a day, doing so only at high noon when the sun is strongest and the eggs can remain warm even in her absence. Once the eggs are cool, they're gone and the hen knows this, so she leaves the nest only under a warm sun's condition and for a short time only. Also, a hen after sitting for twenty-one days is a sorry sight, looking unkempt and a terrible mess, her feathers fallen, colour gone from her cheeks presenting herself in a rumpled manner. This is after twenty-one days with chicken eggs, well, goodness gracious can you imagine what she looks like after *twenty-eight* days of sitting on duck eggs, a full week longer? A full week is a long time when you are sitting on eggs. Even worse, the hen needs to roll the eggs over once or twice a day, and she will do this by bending over and using her beak and neck. This is all right with chicken eggs, eggs of her own kind, but duck eggs are bigger and my poor hen has a heck of a time with them, me needing to help her do it, rolling them over for her. I would put a pencil "X" on one side of the egg; one day the "X" is up, one day it is not. This way I could see if the egg had been properly rolled, or not. Humans are considered smarter than fowl, but is it true? Think of it. The hen did not need to mark the egg with a pencil, to know if she rolled it or not, using her instinct to get the job done, me needing to use a pencil, and so bringing me to wonder, who is more powerful in the brain department, me or the hen. I would give the vote to the chicken.

But putting duck's eggs under a chicken is bad, and not to be done. I will never do this again, my hen almost dead from duck's eggs. Things got worse for the hen after the duck eggs were hatched. Chickens hate the water and will not swim. Ducks on the other hand love water. You've heard the expression like ducks take to water? You have? Good for you. Well, here she is now, on the banks of the creek, her brood of ducklings with her and suddenly they all jump in the water. The mother chicken goes nuts. Get out of the water! You will become drowned! Even worse, the river rats will drag you under and eat you! Get out of there!

See? My fault. This poor hen is going crazy with ducklings instead of chicks, the ducks having an entirely different culture. Never do this. It is mean spirited.

But as time goes by, the ducks grow up strong and fat and the hen turns to other interests and so the ducks are on their own, finding grubs on the river bank, eating grains from river weeds, just generally having a good time, enjoying life.

But wait a minute! These ducks were grown for the market, for the fancy restaurant, for the gourmet customers at the fancy diner. Who is going to slaughter them, for sale? I said to my husband John, who is going to kill the ducks? John said not him, he would not be capable in that area, his area being metallurgy, producing first class goods for the Wallace & Barnes Company, killing ducks was not his department, someone else would have to do that one.

Nor would I put the job to my young boys, feeling it would be wrong to do so, exposing them to the cruelty to animals.

Who would? No one likes to kill. I guess you know the outcome, there was only me to do this. At three months ducks are ready for the slaughter. My ducks were three months old. Time passes, the slaughter put off. Now they are four months old, a month past their prime and still they have not been slaughtered. At five months I know there is no choice, I am required to do this. I choose to do it by Friday, this being Monday and I try to build up my courage and it is not easy. I know how to kill ducks I have seen my Oma do it, telling me to always give a little prayer first when my time came to do as such, since it is written biblically to do this for food. And so she would take the duck and fold back its wings, place it on the ground, her foot on the wings gently, not to break the wings or you will bruise the meat. And now you pull back the head and the duck makes no complaint, he knows you and it trusts you thinking this must be okay, and now you quickly make a cut with a butcher's knife on both sides of the throat just beneath the chin, cutting the main veins and the blood pumps out with each beat of the heart, until the blood is all gone from the animal. This is just awful. As it was for me.

The killing day arrives and I delay the morning, spending time doing little tasks trying to avoid. Later, I go reluctantly to the duck pen where my ducks always come to spend the night in safety, and lift out my first duck. I recognize this one, his mandible is a lighter orange than the others, and painfully, he has been my favourite, my sweet duckling, always so lively and bold, a real rascal, sometimes even pulling at my apron pretending it is food, having a game with me. And this little duck trusts me, seeing me as he had a hundred times before, him feeling no fear, completely confident in our knowledge of each other.

Can I do this? Can I really put him to the ground, fold back his wings and cut? I will at least test myself to begin. I place him on the floor, his wings gently back and my foot on them. Making matters worse, he does not protest, he trusts me. I close my eyes, the sting of tears in them, and in a prayer to Almighty God, I ask why did He make us in this way, the need to kill to live, to actually eat others. Why would you do this? You, the all-powerful, could have made us all to eat just vegetables instead of meat. Why am I in this circumstance at this moment? Why did you give me the ability to love even a lowly duck, and then command me to kill him for food? God, and forgive me for even making the suggestion, if I was the creator of all, this is something that I would have left out.

These are the things I will never understand. Even if I live to be one hundred.

And then, with the tip of the knife I scrape a small depression in the earth for the blood to go, to return his blood to the earth and now quickly I cut his neck on both sides at the main veins, him now trying to protest by flapping his wings which he cannot do being held down as he is. The duck has been betrayed by me and now he knows this, the blood squirting out and onto the dirt as his heart pumps, his blood falling into the little ditch that I had scratched, and me covering his blood with dirt.

And in the greatest of sadness, I do the same to each of the other ducks almost like a zombie I do this, stunned by my own cruelty, until each is dead and in the bushels.

But I will never understand the reason.

39 NOW THE WAR IS OVER AND THAT IS GOOD, BUT coming up with new problems. No longer can I sell pork in a black market way, oh no, pork is no longer on ration, and you can buy it anywhere and I am in loss of all my previous customers, presenting a new problem for me. What to do? Well, goodness gracious, the pork business is gone. I need to find a new way to make money to pay that darned mortgage which is always hanging over my head.

Tomatoes.

Tomatoes for ketchup. Yes, just down the highway there is a ketchup factory and they need tomatoes for ketchup. Everyone loves ketchup. It's ketchup on this, ketchup on that, and the red and sweetly sauce was about to help pay my mortgage. I convince everyone in the family that ketchup tomatoes would be the only way to get enough mortgage money. So we plant tomatoes, the ketchup factory asking us to load those trucks, bring all those tomatoes in, put them on the back ramp, bring as many as you have, we will take them all, we are in the ketchup making business, the public's favourite sauce, they put it on everything and it will always remain popular. So we plant a huge field of tomatoes for the ketchup factory, being twenty thousand tomato plants coming through as a huge field of tomatoes, as far as the eye could see. But wait a minute. It was not then as it is today: there is no machinery for planting tomato plants and all the work must be done by hand, and a huge task, indeed. But hard work never bothered me. I would revel in it. Sweat pouring down off my brow, the sun beating down, from sun's rise to sun's set, was okay with me, my sons complaining of the labour, you're going to kill us with this much work, but keeping up anyway, me bending over in the hot summer's sun, just five feet tall, one hundred and ten pounds and as my Oma would say, like a spark off a fire.

Two months later and what we had done? Look at that field! A field gone green with tomato plants, soon to be dotted with red ripe fruit, twenty thousand plants filled with fruit, a wondersome sight to see.

Twenty thousand times did we bend over
to place a tiny tomato plant in the rich black earth.
Twenty thousand times did we bend over
to place a handful of 7–7–7 type fertilizer around each plant.
Twenty thousand times did we bend over
to hoe each plant, under the blazing sun of summer.
And we cropped these plants in their maturity
sending their tomatoes away
showing up in bottles of ketchup for city people
none knowing the labours of growing them
just that it is thick and sweetly,
making everything taste somewhat the same,
seeming to be an advantage.

* * *

THAT POEM MAKES MUCH MORE SENSE IN THE HUNGARIAN tongue, and at a disadvantage in English, having a poor cadence.

Thinking about it, without that ketchup factory we would have again lost another farm. So, hurrah for the ketchup bottle and might God bless the handsome tomato, as I am sure he does. Yes, and might God bless the ancient Chinese too.

What's the Chinese got to do with it?

Well, just about everything. Yes, those Chinese, always coming up with another sauce, were first with this one too, the rest of the world jumping in saying hey this is pretty good, what did you put in it. The Chinese just giving a smile, saying glad you like it.

And with the money from these tomatoes I paid my mortgage, keeping the sheriff from arriving at the doorstep to read his proclamation, his two assistants eager to begin moving chattels, the children curiously watching, the mother weeping on the porch, the husband away at work. I grew tomatoes for a dozen years and kept that mortgage going. Ketchup tomatoes saved the day.

But the work was so hard that my sons began to plan an easier way of life for themselves. Working this large farm producing all these agricultural goods was hard work indeed. My oldest being Danny, started to work for a dairy, finding that less painful than this. My middle son Johnnie took the easiest way out, turning to a life in the arts, a radio announcer and radio actor first, later a television host, presenting television programs in Toronto, in Cleveland, in Cincinnati, in St. Louis. He had a varied life, meeting important people from around the world, even having lunch with Bobby Kennedy, my asking what it was like, him telling me, well Bobby could have worn a better suit, this one all rumpled. Well, Bobby was campaigning for his brother, not having time to keep himself kempt. My youngest son Glenn, seeing that his brother Johnnie was having an easy time of it in the arts, took up the same interests. Well, they found their own interests, different than mine. They did not have a passion for farming. So the growing of tomatoes came to an end. I was the only one to remain interested. My husband John did not, he liked working for the Wallace & Barnes Company, fashioning steel.

So in following years, these beautiful fields, my passion, went empty.

40 A VERY BAD THING HAPPENED IN THE AUTUMN OF 1964. It started with just a clap of thunder, but not an ordinary clap, this one was so sharp it made the windows rumble and my ears ring in echo. A storm was brewing

as they say, coming into being, beginning to show itself. The skies
darkened until it looked like sundown right in midday. And the
ruckus of the storm in progress brought a strange sense in me,
in my feelings sending me back many years to my trip to Canada
across the Atlantic on the *Belvedere*, in a winter's storm, the noise
so loud you could feel the world coming to its end, the storm
tossing the ship around much as a toy, lifting it higher and higher
and then banging it down into a valley of water, the rear of the
ship rising high into the night air—I can still hear the propellers
racing. This storm now in progress brings a flood of memories
back, feeling real, the memories of a frightened child presenting in
an older woman trying to sit out a late summer storm. Looking out
this window, the storm getting more intense, rain not yet falling,
but a smell of the storm, a smell like laundry bleach, spreading
everywhere. And now it really breaks loose, the trees outside my
window resisting by bending back and fro, until I look down into
the farm's yard and begin to see a few boards go flying off our big
barn and I say to John, scared silly, we are going to lose that barn,
John. Not just a few sticks flying off now, but actual boards are
being picked up and sent whirling in the air. If a few side boards
come off I say to John, once the winds get inside, the whole thing
will go flying apart, it will just explode from the pressures.

And I earnestly complained to him, saying to him, I told you
years ago the east wall is unstable, and is moving inward, each
year another inch or two, the day will be coming when it will just
buckle under the weight of the barn above it, and fall.

John says the trouble with you is that you don't understand
physics. The weight of the barn above will actually stabilize the
wall, holding it down, keeping it constant.

Well, John was wrong about that one, micrometer and slide rule
knowledge not serving him well in this situation because in the
next hour or so, storm in progress, John's physics fail and the barn
blows over. Just came tumbling down. We were stunned.

The features of the barn, once so known to me, suddenly looking strange, crumpled as it was, at the foot of the hill, like a pile of junk, once so mighty now just rubble. It was originally a beautiful bank barn. A bank barn is one that is built on the side of a hill, the first floor in the ground, the hayery and granary above it. Our barn was never painted, keeping the natural look of greying boards, while the foundation was made white with a lime mixture, painted on to discourage spiders and other insects. This was a classic Ontario barn and gorgeous in its simplicity.

Now, it was laid out flat.

The barn's doors that I had opened a thousand times, no longer in their proper entryways, now just flat pieces of shaken debris, the rooms I once worked in and knew so well, mysteriously disappearing in the damage, the huge beams that held the barn erect, now showing skyward. It was unnatural. Our barn is just a winnow of wood.

A sad sight. A dead loss.

And there was no insurance for this. We had fire insurance, but no wind insurance. In shock I said to John, maybe we should put a match on it. Put it to flames. Let it burn. I actually spoke like this. And it would have worked. There were enough electrical wires dangling out there making a fire likely, the wind blowing the flames, changing everything to ashes.

But as you will know, putting a match to it cheats the insurance company. One thing to be said about John, perhaps he is not an interesting husband, a plain fellow is he, but as honest as you can find. Not religious, oh no not at all, but honest was he, and not known to use foul language. Nor did he now, his barn blown to bits. So, he looked at me in a disappointed way, for even suggesting.

Next day, the storm over, we are walking in silence around the damage, now just two old people, him moving slowly, nor am I any longer a spark off a fire, just a tired old woman. Yes old, properly ready for retirement, a lifetime of energy spent on just staying alive.

And now an entire barn gone, the value of the farm diminished by as much. Days later from the window I can see John sitting on some main beams of the barn, the storm gone; sitting for several hours, his dog Sandy beside him, and I don't know what was going on in his mind, nor was it my place to ask. Throughout our fifty-five years of marriage, John would not trust his emotions to me, or with his sons or anyone and so I am standing here thinking, why would he do so now? So why go down there where he is sitting. Really, why should I try? It would be pointless this late. In truth, the only time I saw tears from John was the day he was taken to the hospital while in the last stages of a miserable cancer. Dying as they carried him out on the stretcher, leaving his home for the last time, his eyes were squeezed tight and there were tears on them.

That was the only time.

THE BOYS AWAY. THE BARN IN RUBBLE. JOHN WENT into retirement and I went with him. We sold the farm, the one we had lived on for almost twenty-five years, struggling to make those terrible quarterly mortgage payments, the labours of a lifetime done.

And John made some strange retirement choices. He went shopping for a house. He had enough money from the sale of the farm to buy quite a nice house, but he chose the smallest and cheapest he could find, in the town of Grimsby. A small home, tiny in size, and a plain Jane in every way. I was very disappointed saying to him, why so small John, so plain, after a lifetime of work we can afford better, but I believe the barn blown down made this man very insecure, him putting as much cash into reserves as possible, so that nothing else can go wrong.

For another ten years we lived this way. Simply. And I adjusted to this, lucky for me at least the house was within a city block of Lake Ontario, a fine and beautiful lake, looking as big as an ocean, so big, in the evening on the horizon, the curvature of the earth clearly seen, and I would walk down to the shore to collect pebbles and to fill my time and I was turning my attention to building a stone outdoor oven in the backyard of this house, like those in Becse, where in summer heat the women bake outdoors, air conditioners not needed. To get this project underway I had learned to drive John's old sedan. He could no longer do so, his legs under attack from hardening of the arteries and stiff, and so I was given this independence, to drive the car to the lumber yard picking up cement products, getting advice from the young men there as to how to properly prepare concrete for the building of the outdoor oven, them saying here comes the cement lady again, looks like another cash sale, each of us laughing in a jokey way, enjoying each other's company, the young men of the lumber yard always in a good mood, making me to feel good, too.

So, I built the outdoor oven even while knowing I would never get to use it. There was no good reason to build this fireplace, with all the work needed in doing so, except to find again the familiar feeling of Becse, now sixty years past, but holding here in my heart a feeling that never went away.

And now John's health was failing. No longer in charge of a micrometer, no longer in daily use of a slide rule, retired from a life of metallurgy, he stopped being interested in life in general and would sit silently on the front porch, and I knew not what he was thinking, nor did I feel I had the privilege to ask. His health was failing; he had been hospitalized for his legs, the arteries no longer able to carry through the blood, new arteries were inserted of plastic, I have plastic legs now, he would say, like G.I. Joe and then finishing with a cynical giggle, heh, heh, heh, heh, but while giggling, not enjoying the humour of it at all, just being cynical about it. This was a favourite line of his, pointing at his legs. Look, I am G.I. Joe.

And then, the cancer came, turning out to be the most humiliating kind, colon cancer needing to be handled rectally. My darkest time was to see him going through two surgical operations, the last of which put his bowel movements into a colostomy bag. Know what that is? Well, in cutting out the cancer of the lower bowel, the surgeon puts a hoop and collection bag attached. Know what that means? Someone needs to change the collection bag at least three times a day. Know who had to do that? John is a helpless man, he has no motor abilities, he is useless away from his micrometer and slide rule, and the changing of his colostomy bag falls to me. And it is a terrible task. I will not describe it to you. Even worse than the odour is the humiliation that John must endure, him not even capable of changing his bag, becoming so weak from a lack of appetite, suffering in pain, made small by this illness, all is humiliating to him and unsettling for me. But I do this task willingly, strong in the belief that the one thing those who are dying must have is the knowledge that there is loyalty in this life from someone, not to suffer alone. And so I do as is properly required, him lying sick in bed, and me building my outdoor fireplace, still collecting river pebbles, John dying from cancer.

This is very depleting. And our family doctor, seeing my distress, tells me John must be put into a long-term care facility, where persons other than myself can look after him, or soon, the doctor says, we will both be sick. Both. I resist this, strong in the belief that at a time such as this, deathly ill, John needs to know my loyalty. And I insist to the doctor that I will continue to do this, to look after him, to change those bags, just to prove to him in his dying days, that our promises were kept, in sickness and in health, as was bespoken.

The doctor says do as you think.

But he returns two days later, this doctor, this good man, this physician who still makes house calls, and says to me, for the sake of my health, John should go to a long term facility.

Picking an appropriate time, I try to tell John this, and this is coming out as a total disaster, because when I tell him, he does not answer me, he just stares at me with his lovely brown eyes, only to frown and mumble something I cannot hear. He rolls over to face the wall.

This upsets me thoroughly, I have not been disloyal, I have done everything I could to keep him here, but I have not slept a full night since his illness was diagnosed, up all night am I, tending to his every wish, me wanting to serve in this way. Ours was never a romantic marriage, like Oma with Opa in Becse, but at the very least John and I were honest one to the other, and we were both monogamous by nature, so the marriage was serviceable and in its own way it worked.

So I am bothered, with his removal.

And so I go for a walk down to the lake, that huge, beautiful body of water, so large as to look like an ocean, to again gather a few pebbles, just an old woman alone and about to become even more alone, because I am certain that John will not last much longer if he is moved out, the cancer growing at liberty.

But that's how it is with cancer, always waiting, peering over the healthy cells, looking for an opportunity, the opportunity made available by the intake of improper foods, or air, or living habits. I think improper foods killed John. A bad diet had he, avoiding fruits and vegetables, nothing raw ever, just soft foods, quick to offer another opportunity for cancer cells to leap-frog over healthy cells, to start into multiplying until becoming king and kingdom.

And then the irony of all ironies, when the host dies, the cancer dies with it. Can you imagine? In the end the cancer is killed when the host is killed. None is the winner. So, if life is her purpose, what was Mother Nature thinking?

Later that afternoon the medics come and as they are placing

John on the stretcher, I am in the next room sitting in shock with the full feeling I would not again see him alive. Not ever to express emotion, now he does for the first time. As they carry him out his eyes are tightly shut, choosing not to look at me, and there are tears on them.

He never believed I would agree to this. He never believed that I would allow him to be taken from his home and hearth.

He dies three days later.

I am a busybody. I am always involved. Not to sit back and just let things happen, but to investigate thoroughly, being informed, getting new information. So, picking out a coffin for John, the funeral director gets short with me. John loved cherry wood and so I said to the director, I need a coffin in cherry wood, John's favourite. And I can understand John's interest in this, because cherry wood is indeed beautiful and even rare. Hard to get. The funeral director says John can't have cherry wood, but he can get a wood that is stained to look as such, or he says John can have oak, poplar or ash. I resist all this. Get me the cherry wood. That's what I want, him saying he will try, and in the end he gets me one with cherry, allowing that I am indeed lucky in this case.

Another thing happened: In Europe there is not often embalming, and so I tell the director why do they insist on such this in this country, him explaining that it is popular because the country is so large, travel for relatives, he says, can take days, best to be sure, embalming is necessary. And then, not timidly, but with conviction, I asked about the blood. Where does the blood go? That sacred material in which the soul resides, each of us having a soul, make no mistake about that; it is the soul that creates our conscience, our desire to do good things, the rejection of evil. I am certain that this is so.

So, I ask where does the blood go? He said, in the sewer. What? The blood to the sewer? That sacred substance, given no regard? This is improper. In Becse even the blood of the chicken is given proper respect, the fowl slaughtered but its blood falling into a small cleft in the earth, covered up.

No, he says, into the sewer. I say firmly, never do I want that. He says take it easy lady, it is already done.

42 AS A WIDOW NOW, I WENT ABOUT MY BUSINESS, trying to normalize the condition. I kept the house, not moving to an apartment, and I was now grandmother and great grandmother twenty three times over. The kids are pretty good specimens, healthy and productive, no slackers in this bunch, never unemployed, and their visits are a blessing.

In the yard of my house I have two lovely pear trees of the Bartlett stripe. Autumn is here, the fruit is ready for harvest and many overripe pears had fallen to the ground, beginning to ferment there. Not to waste these fermenting fruits, why not make a little grappa like in the old days. What the heck, I will put that fallen fruit to good use. A word of caution, making alcohol of any kind is illegal and the smell is high when cooking, spreading out into the street, perhaps attracting the vice squad but I felt safe in doing such, since my neighbours being long time Canadians would not recognize the smell, always buying the product in its finished state from the liquor store, never cooking themselves. They would not be familiar with the pungent odour of grappa being made on the kitchen stove, me thinking that there is little chance of Royal Canadian Mounted Police paying a visit, to say things like: hey that's illegal, you are not a licensed producer, we are going to arrest you, we don't care if it is legal in Becse, it is not legal here, tell it to the judge. To prevent such a visit, I will cook the grappa at midnight, throwing a little sugar to burn on top of the stove, which will make everything smell like the baking of cinnamon buns is in progress.

So, I stayed up all that night, cooking my homemade brew, listening to the radio, talking to my cat, having a pretty good time. With morning coming and the cooking finished, it turns out this is an especially potent batch. I place a teaspoon full on the bare kitchen table, and putting a match to it for a test of quality, it burns blue and long, indicating that there is much power in the product. So then I think, what the heck, I shall take some of this newly brewed grappa to my sister Klara. Do you remember her? The one who used to rub my sandwich on her sore, making me to give up on eating it, she getting it instead? You do? Good for you. But even in spite of her misbehavings, we were quite close, she and me more than the others, and I thought a couple of quarts of this newly cooked grappa would be welcomed for the winter months in case of colds, and so I would drive the twenty-five miles to St. Kitts where she lived, offering the grappa as a pleasant surprise, look what I cooked last night, and you are welcomed to have it, careful in using, it is quite powerful.

Transporting illegal grappa in a car is a federal offence with five years in jail.

So, I put two quarts of grappa on the bottom of a bushel basket, carefully covering them with a bunch of eating pears giving things a normal look, placing all of this on the back floor of the Ford, ready for the trip.

If you can imagine it, now I am out on the Queen Elizabeth super highway with cars screaming past me on their way to I know not what. Soon, I notice there is a police car behind me, not flashing his lights or putting on his siren, just to follow me slowly for several miles. This was becoming foolish so I thought I will stop on the side of the road to see what's up.

The officer stops behind me, and comes over to me with my window down, and he asks me where I am going and I truthfully tell him I am going to visit my sister in St. Kitts, explaining that I always to do so at least once before the winter sets in, not liking to drive in snowy conditions I tell him, best to do it now. Well, he agreed, saying best to do it now, the roads can be slippery in winter.

As you know, drivers are usually stopped by police for speeding, but I was stopped for under-speeding, the officer saying that I was going too slow on a high speed highway. This is a fast highway, lady, and a slow car is much like a stopped car, dangerous to others, and would I speed it up a little.

I said sure, would be pleased to do so, and incidentally officer, I grow lovely pears in my back yard, if you would like to reach down into the bushel back there on the floor, you can take a few pears for yourself because I am always glad to offer fruit to those I meet in my travels. He does as such, his finger's tips coming within inches of my illegal grappa, my two bottles of booze intended for Klara. But was I worried? No, certainly not. I was certain there was sufficient fruit to cover the bottles completely and that the good officer would be placed in a good mood at such a sweet gift, saying just to speed it up a little and I hope you have a nice visit with your sister.

When I arrive at Klara's place, presenting her with the grappa she laughed when I told her of my adventure with the police officer and the grappa located an inch from his finger's tips while probing for a good pear. Klara laughed and laughed and laughed saying what a devil I am, even as an old woman I am a devil, not much different that the skinny little kid in Becse, nothing has changed says she, I am always up to something.

I told the same story to my son Johnnie. So after I tell the story, he asks if it would be okay for him to write my memoirs, saying I have had many adventures which would make good reading, and should I move to the city of Waterloo where he lives since I am getting on in years, and he says perhaps he could help in looking after me in my old age. I am reluctant to do this, always enjoying my independence, but he is insistent and I give consideration.

Must say, Waterloo is a very pretty city in Ontario, famous for the making of Seagram's whiskey, the smell of that brew blowing over the city every Wednesday, the scouring of the vats in progress, the smell everywhere and I suppose, the cooking of it legal and well licensed, so in a jokey way I think maybe I have something in common with Mr. Seagram, maker of alcohol too. Maybe I could teach Mr. Seagram a thing or two about changing decaying pears into pleasant grappa. Wouldn't that be the limit?

So it is in Waterloo my son finds me a lovely small house on Belmont Street, an English cottage surely, with a truly wonderful garden in the rear, a rock garden, and looking out the kitchen window I can see the garden in full bloom, and sure enough, there are two pear trees already mature and providing free fruit, guaranteeing much cold and flu medicaments to come. I also planted a cherry tree in the garden, wanting to watch it grow, me having a special affection for cherry trees, with the shiny richly greenly leaf, the bark flecked red and black. When cherry trees give fruit in early summer it is a sign that the harvesting season will soon begin, always a welcomed sign.

And I plant a plum tree too, in honour of the plum boy in Becse, always remembered.

At least once a week my son would come by to take me to lunch and we would have a good time, laughing it up, him having a horrendous, high pitched, cackling laugh, the other diners wondering what's going on here, me trying to control myself but not being good at it, chortling, bending over at the table seat, the two of us making an innocent ruckus.

And he asks if he can write my life down. I ask him why? Is this the reason you have me move to this city, to this new home, so you can turn me into a book? No, he says, it's not for a commercial reason, but that my life is an interesting one says he, full of ups and downs, much as those who might read it, and perhaps an encouragement to others. There is nothing self-proud about talking about the events of your life he says, especially if you do so to share. And perhaps he is right in this.

So, from that day forward, he always brings his note book, sometimes a little tape recorder in his pocket that he plucks on whenever we dine out, at first a distraction, later I forget it even being there as I go on with my life. Once he even catches me singing my favourite song of the 1930s, "Red Sails in the Sunset."

My son Johnnie and I go on picnics under the late summer sun. We will pick up a roast chicken and take it with us for later consumption at New Hamburg Park, setting things out on the provided table, a chequered cloth set down, and the chicken on the plate, and I will say a little prayer before eating it, not just to God in thanks for the food, but to honour the chicken having no say in the matter and deserving this special attention from me. And I offer the prayer up, my son just sitting across from me, smiling, waiting until it's over.

Not to become too talky on this matter but I would also say that too many people claim the chicken as a simple creature. They are wrong on this. I observed the lowly chicken for many years in Becse and also here in this country, and too much the chicken goes unnoticed. If you have interest in these things, take the time to watch the chicken in its natural setting, not in pens as they are kept now, but perhaps in the Mennonite barnyard, in search of grubs and such. Listen to its melodic cackle, low contented tones while she scratches the earth in large strokes, the three fingered foot sending the dirt flying, exposing the catch; well, if ever you are lucky enough to have such a rich experience, I think you would be sending thanks heavenward too as I do, for this noble creature, the chicken. From my own experience, no other creature fancies liberty like the chicken, and now in these days of high production, no chicken has the liberty it loves, just confined in boxes for its full lifetime for commercial purposes. Modern chicken farming is sinful.

And more on this, Americans should listen up: the chicken so loves its liberty that Charles Thomson, back in 1782, the chooser of the eagle as symbol to the United States of America, should have chosen the chicken, not the eagle, if he had given it full thought. The chicken loves liberty, which was the purpose of the American Revolution in the very first place. The chicken would have been a worthy symbol.

And maybe since the chicken is still available and unclaimed by America as a national symbol, perhaps Canada should grab it.

AFTER MOVING TO WATERLOO, FOR FIFTEEN years my Waterloo son and I had a very good relationship. But I began to notice that when at one time he came over about once a week, now he was coming over every morning. I asked him why. He asked me, "Haven't you noticed?"

"Noticed what?"

"Noticed that you are always forgetting your medicaments, and now in your late eighties, unattended high blood pressure can kill, even worse give you a stroke, making you immobile. So that's why I come over every morning."

REFERENCE NO.	DATE	CODE	DESCRIPTION
	06/30/00	BF	
325771	07/14/00	IN	30-APO-LORAZEPAM 1MG TAB
327121	07/21/00	IN	45-VASOTEC 5MG TAB
327122	07/21/00	IN	30-APO-DILTIAZEM CD 120MG
327123	07/21/00	IN	30-ELTROXIN 0.1MG TAB
327358	07/24/00	IN	45-APO-FLUVOXAMINE 100MG
328461	07/29/00	IN	30-ARICEPT 5MG
332179	08/21/00	IN	30-APO-LORAZEPAM 1MG TAB
332188	08/21/00	IN	45-APO-FLUVOXAMINE 100MG
332235	08/21/00	IN	45-VASOTEC 5MG TAB
332243	08/21/00	IN	30-APO-DILTIAZEM CD 120MG
332244	08/21/00	IN	30-ELTROXIN 0.1MG TAB
332903	08/24/00	IN	30-ARICEPT 5MG

At one time the most drugs I took was a cup of Camomile tea. Now look at the list. It's a wonder I know what day it is.
Source: Family Archive.

He was afraid of a stroke wrecking my life, robbing me of my independence. Soon he was coming over twice a day. I asked him, why do you come over now twice a day? He said the medicament was to be taken twice a day, and if it cannot be remembered in the morning, how could it be remembered at night? So I said to him you can telephone to remind me. He replied he has tried that and I forget the purpose of the telephone call even before I hang up.

Now three times a day does he come, and the answer is the same. So many different medicaments am I taking now that they have to be taken three times just to not upset the stomach. I tell him, you cannot do this. I will not allow that much attention from you, to me.

He says, "Have you ever heard of Alzheimer's disease?"

I said, "No, what is that?" Now he explains to me how the mysterious condition of Alzheimer's can affect an older person, starting first in forgetting a few things, ending up forgetting everything.

And lately I have been forgetting things. A lot. But I say to him, "I will not be cared for by a child of mine. Just leave the pills here. You have been taking them with you. Leave them, I will abide by the rules." He tells me he cannot do this, I cannot be trusted to take my medicaments, and if I don't properly take them, there is a stroke in my future.

For the first time in our lives my son and I have a fight about this. I am insistent to look after myself. I always have. I have always been a capable person. I have never needed close attention, not even as a child, and I will not accept it now. I am not becoming weak.

Or is that his thought.

The fight this afternoon is long and weighty. The mother and son have become enemies. His explanation of Alzheimer's has made me to feel inadequate. I don't want any more of this Alzheimer's stuff being talked about. "Just get out of here with that. I can handle things myself, and take your damned fruit with you, too." Lately he had been bringing me fruit everyday. "Why do you bring me fruit everyday?" He says, "Because you have stopped eating anything at all. You aren't preparing meals for yourself," he screams at me, "You are in neglect. Your washroom is filthy, your house is a mess, even your dog goes without food, you forget to feed her just as you forget to feed yourself; you are no longer capable. And you forget to pay your bills, your phone, your electrical, your taxes, I am forever bailing you out from the bills, needing to go over to the main office and pay in cash, them not trusting a payment through the bank anymore, just pay up in cash or it's off. And you just sit on the couch from early morning to late at night, sometimes even in the dark, not turning the lights on, just forgetting every normal thing."

Am I going nuts? Is Alzheimer's just another word for crazy? Just a polite word, everyone just too damned polite to call a crazy person a crazy person.

"Get out of here with that Alzheimer's story, and take your damned pills with you," and in saying, I throw all the pills across the floor from wall to wall, my dog starting to eat them, my son saying, your dog is so hungry now it is even eating pills, and now my son is on the floor picking up all the pills, one at a time, from the bottle I had cast about. And now here he is, on his knees, picking up the pills I have thrown about, a grown man reduced to child, picking up each pill, one by one, and I notice as he is bent over, he is weeping, his tears falling on the floor in front of him. He is beaten by my behaviour, frightened for me, what did he get himself into asking me to move to his city to look after me in my old age, me becoming his responsibility and now all this forgetting business, with Alzheimer's threatened.

And I become vicious to him on his every visit thereafter. Still he comes, now three times a day, me toying with him as to whether I will swallow the pill or not. Making a game of him, playing him for the fool, and only after I am tired of this entertainment do I take the pills, more to get rid of him than to please him. If I take the pill finally, he will get the hell out of here, to leave me to the couch, to sit here dazed, all through the day and into the night, sometimes even sleeping in the same spot, not even moving off the couch. The couch has become my spot on earth.

And as morning comes and I am still here on the couch, sure as anything, I will hear the door becoming unlocked, the key turning and he is back again for more abuse and I hand it out, without mercy.

And because I am eating little else, he brings me protein drinks, telling me it is a milkshake, and I drink it, not for nourishment but only because it is sweet and I want something sweet. And he still brings me fruit every day, and after he leaves, I will eat at least the bananas, packing the rest of the fruit back into a bag and leaving it on the front porch, showing that I don't need his damned fruit. He can just keep it.

But fresh fruit is again brought in. Every day for many months does this charade go on, each time I am getting more vicious, and I know I am ugly in this, but I don't give a damn, I am losing control of my life and to be honest, for the first time in my life I am truly scared. Fear was never a part of my life. I took it all, without fear. On the good ship *Belvedere*, with the waves pounding, the ship so deep into a valley of water that her propellers were spinning in the air, and I felt no fear. I didn't even get seasick. And in all the other events in my life that were dark in nature, I felt no fear. But now I am scared to smithereens.

Why can't I die? Why can't I just stop living? Why am I tortured like this, my brain going, my body still functioning, the heart still beating, the breathing ample.

And then I start with the phone calls to him, over and over again. So many calls to him do I make, and as much as I want to hate him, he is the only one who possibly has some answers for me.

So, I will phone him with, "What's wrong? What's going on? What's happening? I don't belong to myself. I am another person. Tell me, what's going on?"

"Alzheimer's," he tells me.

"You are a damned liar," I tell him. "Not such a thing as Alzheimer's. You are making these things up just to get rid of me. You want to get rid of your mother."

He is quiet on the other end.

On one day he is over here and the fight is really horrible. I slam the back door and go into my garden, pacing back and forth, no longer noticing the beauty of it, the garden that once was so important to me, the garden in which I spent hours, collecting off the weeds by hand, or adjusting the twig of a tree, or cutting the small area of grass with a push mower, all these things become echoes, not real. I could remember snippets but no longer cared for their beauty.

And then I bolt into the house, he is still standing there, and I scream at him, "why can't I die? I am going to do it myself. I am going to take something! I will bring an end to this!"

Saying this was a big mistake. Threatening to take my life changed his attitude toward me. Before this was said, he was doing all he could to keep me in my home where I wanted to be. But pacing back and forth in crazy manner in my garden, bolting through the back door, threatening to take my own life altered my future.

He was giving up on me. And I knew it. Now, I have only myself to trust.

44 ONE MORNING OF THIS TIME, I HEAR THE KEY turning in the door, the son returning for a pill remindering. But when the door opened Dr. Coe, my physician, is standing there, my son behind him just a shadow. What is the doctor doing here? He has no business here. The son has brought him. Disloyal. Letting people in here who have no business in doing so. I will take that key from my son, soon. Not to have strangers coming in here, even before dawn. This is awful.

And the son is just there in the background and saying nothing. He is like a vapour, my son, not even manifest, I would say like a poltergeist.

And now, Dr. Coe comes over to me and looking down at me on the couch, standing too close he says, "Zarah," now a long pause, "I think you are going to need to come with me. I am here to take you to the hospital. We are going to give you some tests."

"What kind of tests?"

"Just tests."

"Tell me what kind of tests. You will not test me unless I am given a full account."

"We need to test how far your Alzheimer's has gone. We are doing this for your own good. We need to know how much to do for you. And we can only give these tests in the psychiatric ward at the hospital."

Psychiatric!

"Yes, Zarah. You are obliged to come with me now because by law I cannot let you stay here unattended since you threatened to take your life, your son told me this. As your doctor, now made aware of his patient saying such, I am obliged by law to act on it, to take tests, to determine how capable you are or are not. I am being honest with you. I have too much respect for you to sugar coat. You need an assessment and that can only be done at the hospital. You can either come with me now or have the police come over here to take you later, but you must go to the hospital, no way around that."

Now I get up from the couch, and go to get a broom, the son still standing quietly in the hall, like a vapour. The doctor wants to take me away and suddenly I see that my home is in a shambles. Suddenly I can see the mess and dirt that was not obvious to me even an hour ago, I can see now. The doctor coming here has brought the condition of my home to my attention. There is mess everywhere. There are newspapers piling up, and me forgetting to let the dog out, forgetting because of many distractions, there are dog deposits. So I take the broom and begin to sweep the floor, awkwardly first, the dog stool rolling in front of the broom, and I am here to try to show Dr. Coe that I am still capable, I can sweep and clean and maintain myself and the dog stool is just an accident and now I am screaming at the dog for what she has done on the floor, screaming to the doctor that this dog is a bad one, badly mannered, and now the dog which has been my faithful friend for fifteen years, in pure anger I kick her. She jumps sidewise and yelping in a confused state, my dog wondering why she deserved this, from me her mistress, and the doctor grabs me from behind by the hands, and tells me to come now, to take it easy, to go with him, and seeing what I have done to my dog, my resolution is weakened, the misery of all the months comes in – kicking my dog until it yelped. Weakened by this action, I do the doctor's bidding and without a coat, just in a dress, powerless, I am helped into his car crying, and taken to the hospital, where very quickly two attendants take me to a room, an unpleasant room, green and airless.

I am furious. No more of this. How can they do this to me? Who has the right? Where is my son? Is he too cowardly to be here? Not the courage to confront? Now he is truly just a vapour.

Is this what I deserve? I have been of service to everyone I have met in my life. I have done my best for my family, for friends, for my neighbourhood even. And this is the reward? Kept as a prisoner, in an insane asylum? Because that's what this is! There are crazies in here! There are young men in here, dangerous looking. And I am given a room with another woman, another European woman, poor soul, displaced too from her European life and gone crazy from it, she pretending to be back in Yugoslavia asking me if there will be perogies for the night meal! And good God, she is here, in this green room, airless.

And I scream at her, you are nuts! You are not in Yugoslavia. You are here in Canada, in a green and airless room! You are in a psychiatric ward. You are nuts. You are of a weak nature. You have no strength.

A day goes by and my son does not show up. Him, who once showed up three times a day with my medicaments, shows up not at all now. He is disloyal. And then the attendant, being asked of this, tells me the doctor has ordered him to stay away since the sight of him riles me so much. The attendant is lying because my rile is not caused by the sight of my son but by what is happening to me, and I tell the attendant, please to have my son come in here, that I am in an isolated state, and if there is fear for my sanity, this being in here will cause more of it, this place can drive anybody nuts.

Now this main nurse says I am here for therapeutic assessment. What the hell is therapeutic assessment, say I. What's going on here?

Well, I am soon to learn what therapeutic assessment is.

They put me in an interview room, and a psychiatric doctor is attempting to interview me. I would say only attempting because this is an impossible event. The psychiatric doctor is of Indian origin, from Calcutta perhaps, his English even worse than mine, and a mumbler to boot. So he is mumbling, the notes and tones warbling even, the sound of an ancient culture still on the tip of his tongue, no matter how long he might have been in this country, he is mumbling to an ancient tune.

And anyway, why isn't he in his own country, serving his own people. Think about it: his own people paid for his training in this field, the rural workers of his homeland paying up the taxes for education, the farm workers and factory workers doing the paying, him doing the receiving, and then he emigrates to North

America. What is he doing here? Just more money. If that's all he wants, how can he be interested in my problems, mumbling stupid questions to me such as: "Who is the president of the United States," the correct answer of which rules me as sane, the incorrect answer puts me in here for still another week. That's how he earns a living, this psychiatric doctor from the Calcutta, whose education was paid for by the poor, and here he is now picking up big cash rewards for therapeutic assessments.

Who is nuts here? Me, or this place of therapeutic assessments?

Now they have placed earphones on me. Earphones are leather-covered pieces fitting over my ears which the doctor speaks into, and they have done this because my hearing is faulty, made worse by the mumbling of the doctor. The hospital has taken these nigglings into consideration, accommodating the bad hearing of the patient and the poor speaking of the psychiatric doctor.

Now the earphones are on me. The psychiatric doctor is sitting at a separate table, and he is a fussbudget, adjusting this, adjusting that, rustling the papers, but not even bothering to even take a look at me. He has other more important things on his mind I suppose; perhaps he is listening to the voices in his head.

There are others in the room. And it begins to make me giggle to see the bunch of us, a United Nations. Just think of it: the patient is Hungarian, the nurse is Oriental, the doctor from India, and now the newest member just arriving, the hospital equipment operator is Trinidadian. Oh, the music of it all! It's like a damned concert in here. It's really hilarious. You should have been there.

And I too would have found all this very amusing if seen as a television play or on a stage, and I am wondering with all this crippled English if I am being understood in my answers to questions like who is the president of the United States, and I am supposing that if you don't know that one, you really are nuts.

So I answer, "Bush." And I repeat Bush over again, in the fear that these people don't understand my answer, their English knowledge in such short supply, and I repeat again as a plus answer to several other questions, stating things correctly and then adding, "Bush." Making sure it is obvious to one and all that I know just who the president of the United States is; yes it is "Mr. Bush."

Now they are saying okay, okay.

But it is not okay. I know what they are up to. If someone doesn't know who the president of the United States is, they must be nuts and they will be held in here, forever. And therefore I have got to get this established, and that's why I repeat that the president of the United States is "Mr. Bush."

I just want to go back to my house, and to my dog and my garden. Away from this place of crazies, brooding young men in a confused state wandering around in here, probably dopers who have destroyed their ability to think, taking in all unhealthy drugs, ruining their bodies and minds, something I have never done, not even do I take in alcohol, except for the grappa sometimes, always plenty of vegetables in my diet which are not available here in the nut house, all the food cooked to a creamy texture in this place, nothing substantial, no knives or forks in the diner either, only spoons, and gee I wonder why that is.

What a conclusion for a life. In the nut house am I. Have I not come a long and terrible way from my child's life in Becse? I am the same person as that little girl in Becse, with Oma and Opa, truly the last love I ever knew, nothing since. And the plum boy, where is he? Or how is now the young sailor on the Belvedere? These remain fresh in my memory so how can this be the dreaded Alzheimer's? I think the idea of Alzheimer's is just an easy diagnosis for the psychiatric doctor, just to say this is Alzheimer's or that is Alzheimer's. Well, I know what's wrong with me. I am just depressed and for good reasons. No need of therapeutic diagnosis. Depressed because life is too hard for everyone.

Not Alzheimer's. I think my memory is perfect. My memories of my youth are in perfect condition, my childhood in the village of Becse cannot be taken from me, I remember still, getting up early in the morning before my siblings, the dawn just breaking, just to be with my Oma, to race her to the market, doing anything to be in her company, my love for her so high. I can dip into my memories anytime I want, the Alzheimer kept at bay, I relive my life with no interference. And in the dark of night as I lie awake on my cot in this place, in my imaginings I return there. In the dark anything is possible. My feelings have not changed one bit in all these years, only my appearance has changed, almost ninety, the skin in a loose state about my face and throat and sometimes in a wonderment, looking in the mirror I will pause to look at myself, peering at the eyes, the mouth, the chin, and I whisper to myself: "Is that you Zarah? Is that you? Are you a survivor, Zarah? Or are you just a debris?"

My face is old. Almost ninety years on earth. And I have taken on the look of age. Where once there was a youthful beauty, skin pulled tight, the legs thin, the face olive and healthy looking, replaced now with a wrinkled circumstance. Too many disappointments I believe comes out in the skin, oh yes it does, showing up first in the brow, causing a furrowing, the frown doing damage all the way down to the toes, even the toes in a wrinkled state, taking away the appearance of youth, presenting a different person entirely. But spooky it is, because with all these outside changes, all this deregulation, the old woman still remains a youngster beneath it all, only the outside is changed, I am the selfsame person. Still a kid.

Now the psychiatrist and nurses are saying, "Zarah, you are dozing. Just answer the doctor's question."

I tell them I have already answered.

It is "Bush."

JIGSAW PUZZLES AND HOW'S YOUR BOWELS. These are the main questions here. Soon after you arise in the morning, they will take you to the games room, and the whole bunch are sitting there, some talking in a foolish way, others playing pinochle, or a game of fish, and they give me a jigsaw puzzle, which they give to anyone whose English is not the mother tongue, convinced are they, that the foreigner cannot understand the English going on, and jigsaw puzzles require no word knowledge, forgetting that I can handle three languages, Hungarian, German and English, but still I am offered just a jigsaw. I am trying to fill my time with the puzzle while awaiting my son, who the nurse says will be coming for visit, this being his first since I have been put here by Dr. Coe who is responsible for all this nonsense.

So, I say to the main nurse, "I have been working on this jigsaw for several hours, and I am sure there are parts missing and the missing parts are driving me crazy."

Me using the word "crazy" puts a wry smile on her face, as will other words such as "nuts" or "wacko." These words spoken by a patient in a psycho ward always brings a smile to hired help.

That's what the patients call the nurses and doctors here, the hired help.

But she says, "Oh no this is a new puzzle, you can tell by the catalogue number on the back of it, see here the date printed means November and that's what this month is."

And I say to her, "Is this some kind of secret way to determine if a person is crazy or not, if not to complain of missing jigsaw parts and just fruitlessly keeps on trying, she is nuts? If she complains of missing parts, asking where are they, she is on the mend? Is this similar to the question asked, who is the president of the United States? Not knowing keeps you in here while knowing the correct answer gets you out?"

"Nothing of the kind," she says, "nothing of the kind." And now she moves to the second most often asked question, how are my bowels doing, if in a constipated state, they have a product I can take, and don't suffer in silence, many of the medicaments given here have a constipating effect, which she says can be put right. Constipation, she says, is no fun.

I tell her my bowels are darn near perfect. You should be so lucky.

That's how it is in here. I am having trouble keeping the days straight. I don't know the date, the only calendar is in the nurses' station, the number kept secret, nor is there seen a timepiece, so every day runs into the other. I am visited daily by a psychologist, no longer by the psychiatrist, psychologists being more economical doctoring, keeping down the cost I suppose. And the psychologist is a new kid on the block, not much more than a student, and very bookish, working out the list of human ills. He asks about my childhood, which has little to do with my depression now, or my Alzheimer's, which I do not believe exists, I am just depressed for goodness sakes, and anyone would be, ripped from their home for just saying I will kill myself, not meaning it really, but taken as a serious statement. What did my son expect I would do? Drink a glass of lye? Sure, that has been done by others. All is required is a glassful of water with a tablespoon of the lye in there, swallowed quickly, bringing on a huge hemorrhage in the stomach and certain death. One woman I knew did this, she lived in Caistorville, her dear heart so broken by a nasty husband and not able to speak English, isolated in that house for so many years, she could no longer continue, and so took a glass of lye and brought it to an ending.

So, did my son suspect I would do as such? I think he is the one who is crazy. He is the one who should be in here. Him supposing I would drink a glass of lye after he left that afternoon, when I was walking back and forth in the garden saying I would kill myself, my depression so deep that I could barely tolerate it. That's where I went wrong. I should never have said I would do as such, just done it. Just get it over. Have you ever felt like this? Like you do not belong to yourself in your own skin? Like you have another self? And that other self is a complete stranger?

Everything is disjointed and I have no answers, just that everything seems wrong. And do you think I have Alzheimer's if I can remember these events? Oh, they will say, there are different levels of Alzheimer's, that's what they tell me while they attempt to look wise but understanding nothing, giving answers of questionable quality, knowing nothing really.

I put the doctors to a test. I ask them a simple question: Am I crazy? None can provide a simple answer, yes you are, or no you are not. Like everyone else they just muddle through, these doctors gone bored with their occupations. And I would think, if these highly trained doctors have no answers, why should I remain in an institution with no comebacks? What is to be accomplished with the asking of questions but just coming up with, well the human mind is a complicated thing. You want to know what I think on this? It's just a money maker. That much is obvious.

I just want to go back to my house on Belmont, to be left there, and forget about medicaments or visits from sons or doctors, just to be left alone. I am capable. I promise I will eat proper meals, oh, I promise. And I will keep a neat house, I will do mending as required, and I will walk my dog down the boulevard every day, just a mutt is she, that I picked up at the dog pound because she jumped up in her steel cage the moment she saw me, as though to say, hello there, where have you been, I have been waiting for you, we are meant for each other. She has been my companion for fifteen years now and I promise I will not neglect her. And I will bring my life back to a normal condition as it has been for many years, being almost ninety does not mean you are incapable to live by yourself, if you have the smarts, and I never was a dummy.

* * *

WANDERING THE HALL I LOOK DOWN AND I SEE MY SON HAS arrived and there is some fuss. I am standing in the midway and he is at the other end. I am surprised to feel no emotion. I should be pleased to see him after all this time but I am not. And he has his wife with him; they both have come. What's the occasion for God's sake? What's this all about? Why did she come too? I would have been pleased to receive them at home, but I don't want them to see me here with these crazies, these sour individuals, and I turn to walk away and the nurse says don't you want to see your son, you've been asking after him, and now he is here, don't you want to see him?

And I tell her no. I am humiliated by my being in here, my face burning at the thought of his wife, especially, seeing me in this weakened condition, me in a nut house for God's sake, and away from normalcy, me who has always been so capable, reduced to a child. You, nurse, tell them to go, get them out of here before I scream.

And I can see from the side of my eyes, the dutiful son being told my message just turns around in a walk toward the exit.

And now I am truly alone.

46 NOW IT IS SEVERAL DAYS LATER, I DON'T KNOW the exact number with no calendar or timepiece, but several days later the main nurse comes to me as I am sitting in this gloomy green room, and she says something like, we will be having a meeting of residents at three this afternoon and we would like to include you.

And I say to her something like, why even ask? I am going to go somewhere? Perhaps I am going to go shopping or something and oh excuse me I am sorry but I have another engagement and therefore I cannot attend.

The nurse ignores my sourness and just keeps looking at her clipboard, the one she carries out of a secret importance, saying well we will expect you to be there. I said fine, you know where I am.

I know this is impolite, this sourness. But you can say anything you want around here with no reprisal. These professional people walk around unsullied, accepting the insults from patients like what would you expect, these are nuts and that's why they carry on as they do.

Later this afternoon, she shows up again saying, "The meeting will soon begin."

"What is the purpose of this meeting?"

She says, "So all can share problems, so that none feels isolated."

What do I have in common with dopers and drunks on the mend, or that Yugoslavian lady who has her own problems. I am almost ninety. These other people are children. I don't need to hear their problems. Theirs will never be mine. I have been pulled from my home. I have been taken from my garden and my dog and daily habits. Just get me the hell out of here and I will mend.

"No," says the nurse, "you must attend."

Now we are sitting in a circle and each is given a stenographer's pad, the kind with the spring spine, and a nubby pencil, a pencil of quarter size so it can't be used as a weapon I think, just precautionary move by the hired help, an attempt to avoid problems.

So, we sit, pads and nubby pencils. The doctor has arrived and seats himself in the circle too, and the main nurse has seated herself separate to one side. I am the first to speak saying that everybody ought to put out their cigarettes, the stink in here is too much to handle. Patient #3 says he can't do that because smoking is his right.

Patient #5 agrees with him, saying smoking being a way of handling frustrations the doctor says he has, which he must resolve if he expects to have any personal peace. Patient #1 agrees with me that the smoke in here is too much and ends his opinion by saying he is a smoker, but still would like the cigarettes distinguished.

But I have obvious influence. They put their cigarettes out, each with the ashtray provided that has the plaid bag attached, the kind that cannot tip, the only kind they have in here and the smokers carry one around and when seated place it on their knee and they are seen with it at all times, into which they toss their cigarettes.

I say to them, thank you.

One says much obliged.

Another says he might light up again but for the moment okay.

How can I have Alzheimer's when I can remember such details. I remember every detail if given the time. I cannot recall in an instant, but thinking about it, I can put things in order. If I forget a word or name of importance, I try to recall using the alphabets, going A B C until I get it. This is no Alzheimer's that I have. What I have is a fear that I will lose my independence with too much interference from others, and I was just kidding about drinking the lye, my son should have known better, except to panic to tell Dr. Coe, and now I am in here away from my home and my garden and my dog and my walk up Belmont Boulevard on a cool evening, my dog at leash's end, smelling this or that, stopping at trees along the way, but not even peeing under these circumstances, my dog so polite, she is so reserved. And people stop to talk to me, seeing me daily as an oddity perhaps at my age, but that's okay, we are all in this together and if they gain pleasure from talking to a relic, fine. Those were happy times for me, now taken away. Or when my son would take me for lunch, the chicken excellent, with a nice baked potato perhaps, and a little soured cream on the side, lunch finished with a cut of lemon pie and a cup of coffee. And then at meal's end, to conclude a perfect afternoon we would take a walk in Queen Victoria Park. Here can be seen a bronze statue of Queen Victoria, gone dark in colour but still shiny, in this case she is sitting on a lion.

She probably never did, the sculptor taking leave of his senses in an artistic way, much as my father, the poet, the sculptor shut away from the real things in life, patronized by the rich, who wish to have the same talents, but not.

Now I am giggling to myself thinking of these things and #4 says you are laughing at us. I said no, I have my own thoughts and sometimes I find them amusing, but don't flatter yourself, this had nothing to do with you. Oh yes, he said it is obvious that you are laughing at our predicament, that we are contained in here and there is no way out.

But now the doctor adds his two cents worth by saying yes there is a way out, best to talk about our problems and discover that everyone has them, that none has been singled out or persecuted by circumstance, to which I tell the doctor that I have been persecuted by circumstance more than once dear sir, and how's about that time when soldiers were shooting at our peaceful houses in Becse, as is the case in almost every war, the soldiers perfectly safe, the civilians getting the brunt. I doubt if you know what you are talking about sir, plenty of people of innocence are persecuted, and how can you, training or not, know what each individual here has suffered; these people are damaged goods.

The doctor is shocked by my mouthiness. Now, now, he says, a war is something different, there could be exceptions in that case, but here in North America, most persons are in charge of their own lives.

Not if you use drugs, says #4.

It's your choice says the doctor, to use drugs or not, oh no says #4, the demons are in charge here, they run my life. I do not use drugs, I would rather *ignore* the drugs, but the demons *want* the drugs, and that's why I take the drugs. Are you taking drugs now, says the doctor, no I am not says #4, but the moment I get out of here I will get myself another contact right away, to satisfy the demons, not at all for myself.

That's when I added that the demons within him is really the devil and they should all become Jehovah's Witnesses, me saying this shocked the nurse so bad she actually yelped.

Religion has its place, this is the doctor talking again, religion has its place in these things such as in the twelve steps of AA, but for many the strength must come from a rational understanding of the problem and that's what he is here for.

So, this nonsense went on for almost two hours by this time I am tired of the whole thing and everyone else must have been too, because one by one they sneaked from the room, heading for the exit in a stooped manner, bending over as they walked, making themselves smaller, pretending not to disrupt this very important meeting and they would be back after attending to some personal business, but they never came back.

Ended up with only the nurse and the doctor in the room, going over their notes in a very professional way.

THEY HAVE ADJUSTED MY MEDICAMENTS. That's how they inform me that I can go home. They are convinced they have done much good with me, the main nurse saying that I have made great strides since being brought in here, with me thinking nothing has happened ma'am, I still do not feel like I belong to myself, but I just ask if my son is coming to pick me up, or perhaps I will walk. "Oh no, oh no," says the nurse, "I spoke to him and he will be here."

The dutiful son arrives, and I am not pleased to see him since he has been part of the plot. Each worked to put me in the warehouse, putting looking after me, aside. There is an old Hungarian saying, mother can give care for five children, five children cannot give care for one mother.

So, they motor me home, me in the back seat, and good, this ride is beginning to return me to a normal world, to see people walk, a lady pushing her baby buggy, and I think to myself, what is going to become of that infant, will her life be peaceful or will she have a tough time of it? All lives are difficult, even the Greeks saying so. But if this was properly recognized there would be no conflict in the world, no wars, no abuse, each saying, gee this is a tough road we are each given, we are all going to be battered on this road, no one gets off without widespread damage, not even the rich, not even the smart, not even the artist, so let's all give a little help to each other. Perhaps even the rich lowering their arms to those below saying, "I have been fortunate in both intellect and finance, I will bend over to help you and we will dull the sorrow soon to be handed out to each."

But people hand out abuse to each other almost like misery to the other is like one of life's prized trophies.

Yes, suppose there was just such a trophy, a Life Trophy, a thousand feet high, with each person's name engraved on it, each person recognized as a Life Survivor, a valued participant, each person given the right to say, I am a survivor.

Or maybe grave markers are these! Yes, that's it! Just thought of it. That's the trophy we are granted after living a long and thorny life being a granite grave marker with our name on it giving both the birthing date and you guessed it, the expiry date. But I have come to notice grave markers are no longer in general use these days. Now, it's just burn him up and put the cinders in a jar with, *He Was Beloved By All Who Knew Him*, and give him a niche in a mausoleum. Do you agree? Perhaps you do.

I look around and I am glad to be home but there are awkward moments as my son moves to leave me alone here for the first time in some while. He tells me he is pleased to see me back, but standing at the door, ready to depart, already begins the imposing, saying he will again need to visit three times a day, the pills being the reason, and no argument about this, please. Already we are in disagreement. I inform him that I am perfectly capable of looking after the taking of pills and also I don't want any domestic help coming in here to do things. Well, he says we shall see.

Good. He is gone.

* * *

I HAVE LONG CONVERSATIONS WITH MYSELF.

"Is that you Zarah?" I am looking into the mirror in the washroom in the half dark, and I am addressing my image. "Is that you Zarah. Are you the selfsame person? Where did you drop the ball? Now almost ninety years, what has happened to your intellect? What is this Alzheimer's? Or is it as I suspect, just a general explanation by the psychiatrists, psychologists, psychotherapists, each just guessing. Or perhaps you, Zarah, are out of place on this planet, ignoring the practical, taking life to a lyrical level, all the mile markers gone."

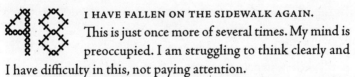 I HAVE FALLEN ON THE SIDEWALK AGAIN.
This is just once more of several times. My mind is preoccupied. I am struggling to think clearly and I have difficulty in this, not paying attention.

Here is the list of falls: I have fallen while walking my dog on Belmont. I have fallen leaving the bank. Once I even fell while my son had taken me to a physiotherapist to relieve the pain of a previous fall. But this morning I have fallen down the steps, crashing through a glass door, not cutting myself thank you God, but sending the glass into smithereens, all this happening unfortunately while going to answer the door, my son coming through and seeing the damage, silently cleaning it up, and what was going on in his mind, seeing this?

Other mischances too. Once, I left the upstairs tub to running into an overflow state, eventually the water running out the bathroom and down the stairs. Unfortunately, I didn't notice the wet, not even though my house slippers are soaked; I am occupied with other thoughts, my son coming in on a pill journey, seeing this flood on the floor, me walking around in it, needed to call a plasterer, the ceiling in the living room of my lovely cottage now in a fallen condition.

So, all these events added up. The end is near. My son is asking if I would be interested in moving into a retirement home, best for me he says, with daily attending by a willing staff, and I tell him no. Then, he says, I will build you accommodation in my house, a full separate place. I tell him no, I will not live with a son; I will continue to live by myself. Ignoring my wish on this, he proceeds to build me a place at his house and after two months it is finished. He asks me to go see it, to see if it is appropriate, to see if I would like to live in it, and so he drives me to his address.

Oh my goodness! He has even prepared tea for me. So gracious! So gentrified! He has placed a table for two at one end of the very large central room of the new apartment, at the window, choosing a beautiful sunny afternoon for the showing. If you would now ask, I could not describe what this apartment looked like. I can recall nothing of it, excepting that it was quite large with a modern kitchen of cream and green. I am taking no notice of it, just to tell him no, thank you very much, but no anyway.

He is disappointed but he should not have foolishly gone ahead and prepared. Well, some old women enjoy such attention, but that is not my makeup and he knows this. I do things on my own. I always have. I do not need another conducting my day like an old Budapest grande dame.

Not accepting the dutiful son's apartment put him into talking about a retirement home again. I did not know this at the time, but the wheels were already in motion, with different individuals coming in to interview me, on what kind of retirement home I would like best and squeezing my brain for all it was worth. I made it appear to them that indeed I was entirely capable, that some people are just as capable at ninety as others at fifty and that a retirement home is out of the question with somebody like me.

I explain this to these young interviewers, looking them immediately in the eye and indicating that not only am I able to keep my house going, I have also built a very large pebble collection, pebbles of every description, little flakes of granite on this little pebble or that, beautiful all, I should have been a geologist or gemologist, or something. I love these stones. I take the young interviewer to my garden and show her the vast collection on display there, the ones next to the tiger lilies, and then an even larger collection of pebbles, most gathered from the railway tracks, the tracks being a trove of such.

And now the interviewer seems to become very interested too, bringing her face up close to mine, the pores of her fleshy face large and yawning, becoming distorted, the face of an inquisitor really, this woman who has come to take me from my things, my pebbles and my garden, and my gorgeous tiger lilies too, which were leftovers at first, brought in after being thrown out by others, put by the weekly garbage on a side's street. I picked these up and gave them a new life, a new opportunity, and now look how much appreciation they have given back to me, all bright and orange, as if to say thank you, thank you for giving us another chance and we will show our appreciation in this by working hard to provide much pollen for the bumble bees of your garden to load up and take home.

Can you see the interdependence here? Of course you can. Can you see how my life on Belmont is woven into all things? And now the threat of being taken away to some retirement home because I am accused of Alzheimer's, where the inmates doze, seated on Lazy Boy chairs, mouths gaping in sleep late into the afternoon, and in the deep of the night, can be heard the snores of a thousand, each day meaningless while awaiting the black buggy, much like the black buggies of Becse, those of the sedan type pulled by four black horses, with a black-caped driver, taking the Dead Ones to the cemetery.

The Dead Ones never leave us. My Oma and my Opa are as alive as ever.

I am spinning back to Becse, eighty years past, and as clear as yesterday, the bullets bouncing off walls and threatening each of us, the sound of the discharge loud, Oma, the bravest soul I ever knew, shaking like a leaf holding onto her grandchildren beneath the bed, our parents away, gone to the New World to establish a new life, and she and Opa trying to keep things normal, while outside platoons of brave soldiers shoot the homes of innocent villagers.

I am just kidding when I call them brave.

These men were poor excuses.

49 MY DUTIFUL SON IS A COMPLAINER. HE WILL SAY to me, why do I remain on the couch every day, not even going up the stairs to bed at night, just remaining in one spot, here on the couch, waiting for time to go by. Why?

I don't know. And when I am not doing this, I am calling him on the telephone to ask the question, what is wrong here? What's happening? Why do I not feel that I belong to myself? My interests have gone. What's wrong? I call over and over again, getting no satisfaction from him, or anyone else. None can give me a satisfactory answer. Seems to me that my body is still alive but my head is buzzing. They sometimes tell me that this is Alzheimer's and I tell them it is just old age, things out of whack. I tell them as good as my physical health is, my brain is not doing too well, and I am not as smart as I once was, my head veering in and out of solid thinking. So I will tell them I am not into Alzheimer's, I am just dumber from old age. And they will say oh no, you are not dumb, just that you have Alzheimer's disease. Well, to be honest, if I have a choice, I will choose dumber from old age instead of the Alzheimer's. Why? At least dumb is not a disease. And I am thinking, gee, it is strange how old age is now explained away, just by naming it Alzheimer's, the professionals saying now we've got it nailed down, its Alzheimer's, sure, that's it.

We have it identified. Congratulations on us.

My dutiful son is distressed, telling me things have got to change and I cannot be allowed to sit here on the couch day into night, not even undressing for bed, that things must become normalized in my life or I will need to go to a retirement home, where there can be assistance for an old woman with Alzheimer's.

This brings on conflict. Sadly, things between the two of us have become strained. No longer will I agree to go out with my son as for fifteen years I did, perhaps eating a chicken at a our favourite restaurant, entering a greenly park on a sunny afternoon, our conversation filled with jokes. Examples, me retelling events about his father, my husband John, not that John was a bad person, but that he was just a dull man. When he died I bought a duplex grave, one side for him, one side for me, me saying to my son in a jokey way as we walk in New Hamburg park, when they put me down there beside him, have him stay on his own side, let him give full attention to his micrometer it was always his main interest anyway, my son and me laughing at the picture of it.

Yes, and along with the double grave, one side for him and one side for me, I bought a duplex gravestone too, with a space for engraving, which I tell my son, we should write on it, in John's honour these words similar to what Mr. W. C. Fields, the Hollywood film comedian has on his gravestone: *I Would Rather Be In Philadelphia,* which is a joke meaning that Philadelphia was bad enough, but gee this grave is even worse. That's the joke. So in a similar way on John's monument to say, *I Would Rather Be At Wallace & Barnes.* That's the joke. Meaning of course, it would be better.

* * *

AND AS WE WALK HERE IN NEW HAMBURG PARK ON THIS SUNNY afternoon, I begin to softly sing...

> Red sails in the sunset
> Way out on the sea
> Oh, carry my loved one
> Home safely to me...

(Kennedy/Williams 1935)

And on these sunny afternoons I would ask my dutiful son, why did you move me to this city with you, I am a handful, I know I am, I am not an easy person, I know I am not.

And he would say, I have met a lot of people in my life Mother, in the business that I have been in, every kind of famous person, celebrity to politician. Almost every one. Sure, some were cabbages and some were kings, but most were pretty routine. But you Mother, you never bored me.

And that was enough for me.

So, we had many good times together and that's what is so sad about it now, with the Alzheimer's. Once was, when we would cross a busy street, he would reach for my hand in a protective way, which I would refuse because I would say to him, me being so much older, us holding hands, persons will think you are a gig out with an old woman. Which would make him laugh even more especially if I use a modern word like chick. Or if I said awesome about something and that would bowl him over. And then I would have to walk faster in front of him, saying nothing because by this time I think he's going to have a heart attack from laughing, especially if I said cool.

If I used the word cool, that one would almost kill him.

That one was the worst word.

And then, still with my dutiful son, he arrives one morning to tell me that I must go to see Dr. Coe this morning. Why, I ask. Just because, he says. Just because is not a complete answer I say back to him. He says I need my annual check up. Now comes a long argument. I tell him I have no need for Dr. Coe, that I am in perfect health, that there is too much minding of my business by others. But I am not being truthful in this. Secretly I know I should have the annual check up. I am teasing my son, being cruel really, giving him flak, playing him along. But the question must be properly asked: why do I purposely antagonize my son as I so often do? I tried to figure that one out. Why? That is the *really* interesting question. Would it be that if I make a fuss I can still feel in control of my life, since my life is so controlled by others? Is that the reason? This terrorizes me, this loss of control. I have always been a thoroughly capable person all my life, and now receiving no regard for that, being ordered about by others, even if well meaning. It comes out as humiliation.

So after a good amount of tugging back and forth, I eventually agree to go to Dr. Coe's office for the check up. And I am asking in retrospect, what the heck is he going to check anyway; so skinny and wrinkled am I, there is nothing left to check. But I go upstairs, returning with my coat indicating my willingness.

We arrive at the doctor's office and suddenly I am horrified. Sitting on those chairs with a dozen other patients, I notice, dear God, I have not dressed. Beneath my outer coat is my nightie, making me next to naked in a public place. Just a flimsy thing of chintz is this nightie. But I love fabric. I love chintz although chintz is into a bad reputation, the word chintzy meaning cheap. And cheap it might be, a polished cotton fabric made to look like silken cloth. See? I know about these things. I care about cloth. The history of it. Ordinary cloth is a marvel.

But a nightie is not to be worn to a doctor's office for a check up. What will he think when he sees this? Just it will confirm Alzheimer's. So, I say to my son, let's get out of here. He refuses. He got me this far, he is not going to surrender now. I tell him I am not properly clothed, I have on just this nightie. He says its okay, Dr. Coe has seen nighties before, this will not be the first one he has seen, a nightie is just a nightie. And then, I say to him, sure Dr. Coe has seen nighties, you are correct with that one, but never in these circumstances because if he saw nighties it would always be under private circumstances, as a husband and wife, for goodness sakes, not decked on an old woman like me.

Suddenly, I notice everybody here in the waiting room, on hearing much of this, is trying to avoid laughing. Smiles all around. Some with their magazine held up to their faces their shoulders shaking in silence; some pretending to adjust their shoelaces, their faces down in the direction of the floor. And now I am terrorized. Scared to my death. Soon I will lose respect completely. A laughing stock.

The faces of the people here in the waiting room are suddenly fuzzy to my eyes, and I am here wishing them away. I squeeze my eyes shut and wish deeply; as deeply as I did when I was a child in Becse when events were displeasing, when horrible things were happening in my childhood's universe. And the wishing works! After all these years, the deep wishing still works. Away they go! The waiting room is emptying. I watch it change, becoming not much more than fog. The room is empty! The antagonists are gone. In a muffled sense I hear much commotion. The doctor is summoned and by this time because I am lying on the floor.

They told me later it was hyperventilation. I think it was humiliation.

50 THIS MORNING UNUSUAL THINGS ARE IN progress. I hear a rap at the door and when I open it a friend I have not seen in twenty years is standing there. She has always been a best friend, but over the years, time and distance separated us, and now suddenly, for no reason, Valerie is here on my doorstep and I pass to her a warm hug, glad to see her again. But standing behind her is my number one son, Danny, and his wife has come along too. Only Johnnie the dutiful son is absent. What's going on here? For what purpose on this sunny morning they have come? Did I misinvite them?

"Hurry," Valerie says to me, "hurry, let's get you dressed and go!"

"Go where?" I ask, "I believe this is a reasonable question."

"We are going back to your old town for a long visit. The town you lived in before you moved here."

"Long visit? To the town of Grimsby? How long? Why? I like my home here. I have been here for many, many years. Why would I need a visit extended elsewhere?"

"You will have a good time in Grimsby. Lots of fun. In your old town you have many grandchildren to visit. Here you have just Johnnie and his small family. It is lonely here for you."

"Well," I tell her, "I will go for a visit. Sure, I will be glad to do that, since I have nothing on the line for this morning. Sure, I will be pleased to go as long as the visit is not too long."

But there is a rush going on this morning with these three, something smacks me as not being right. Here they are, moving me along at a hectic pace, to dress, and get ready to go.

"I have not yet fed my animals, my dog and my cat, my companions," I tell them. To my cat I give canned food but my dog likes a special mash made freshly for her, from kitchen scraps prepared to perfection with both cooked vegetables and meaty pieces mixed into oatmeal, plus enriched whole milk thrown in too, and good for her bones.

I have not yet cooked this up for her and my visitors would have me leave this instant. So, I tell them no, I won't go until my responsibility to my animals is done. They will just have to wait. And everyone sits in the living room in silence, all the excitement runs out, as I work in the kitchen slowly making the dog's gruel. The cat gets her food, which she likes in completeness, but my dog is a different matter, requesting a proper breakfast each morning prepared. She has grown accustomed to this and I am always pleased to feed her.

My dog is Sue. She is a lonely animal coming up from the dog pound, none other wanting her. In her last day of the seven day stay until the needle, none came for her, but when she saw me, there was immediate eye contact. She yelped in her cage, standing on her back legs, as though we had met in an earlier time, and now we were together again, aren't we lucky in this, what a happy life is in store for us, this will be wonderful. That was the feeling she put on by her jumping and yelping, by this dog, quiet by nature, but now excited by the prospect of coming home with me. But that is not how it ended. My son tried to discourage me from taking her from the pound at the time, her not having obvious beauty, a mongrel, *very* mixed lineage, I would say a partly Terrier and partly Chihuahua, a homely mixture, but I claimed her a beauty.

Still trying to get his own way, my son said I would look eccentric walking this small strange looking dog on a string, up and down beautiful Belmont Avenue, street spectators finding a comedy in it, just look at that unusual twosome. Wouldn't you know, later that day my son's wife went back to the dog pound and picked up this selfsame dog and brought her home to me, where I broke into tears upon seeing her again. We became a fixture, she and me, as we take our daily stroll, a skinny old lady almost ninety, and her dog now into her fifteenth year, her age showing in her coat, dull looking she is, toted on the end of a string, both specimens ready for the bone pile. It was my son's wife, bless her heart, who finally got this wonderful dog to me after my son convinced me to leave it at the pound. The two of us, joined by fate, two peas in a pod, and she has become my best friend ever since. I would say Sue and I are a mutual admiration society.

And there is my cat. Not that I love my cat less. But she is her own personality. She is an independent one, not currying favour, just being independent. She is named Booty. I call her that because when she walks away from you, the white of her back legs looks so much like a pair of pirate boots. These would appear as Wellingtons, which my father described as the jackboots of the gentlemen of Napoleon's time. So for this good and proper reason, I originally named her Jackboots, but over time it came out Booty alone. So, that's what she looks like in walking away from you. Like a darned pirate. What a dickens is that cat! I bought her for five dollars from a pet store closing down in Waterloo Square. Think of it, my cat was a clearance item. What better thing can you get for five dollars! A living creature, with a personality. Wow! What good fortune!

Now I plate my cat her food and begin the cooking of a meal for my dog, while the newly arrived visitors in the other room are squatting in silence. Making this meal for my dog gives me time to think. There is something suspicious going on here. Why the sudden visit from Valerie after all these years, she taking control of matters, telling me to dress, get ready, we are going?

They are urging me to hurry it up. Some are in the kitchen watching my dog gulp it down, saying complimentary things about my dog, saying don't worry she is a beautiful creature, your son, the dutiful one, will take good care of her.

I tell them no. This dog is my responsibility. And my cat. I have always attended them, they are a family in kind. I know their personalities. They are human to me in every way but speech.

They share my bedroom. The dog is my alarm clock. At seven each morning, I am still asleep, she will start to wake me. First just endlessly walking around the bed, her nails click-click-click-clicking on the hardwood floor. And then giggling to myself, hearing her, I pretend to still be asleep. Now, she makes more noise, her tail whisking back on the floor, hitting the clothes hamper, bang, bang. Still I pretend to be sleeping. Teased long enough my dog will go into the whimpering phase, telling me, get up, get up Zarah, get out of that bed, a new day has dawned! The sun is already on the rise! There is a garden to walk, there are pebbles to be collected from the bed of the railroad tracks. The day will be loads of fun, and surely the walk on Belmont awaits us. Time for the show to begin!

And then, perhaps in competition for my attention, my other animal, my cat does her stretch at the foot of my bed, her mouth into a yawn, appearing like a miniature fierce tiger in the half lighted room. And I am made happy by these two wonderful creatures, who are not intellectual geniuses at all, but the Good Lord gave them just enough brain, not too much, just enough. By the same stroke, I am thinking, the Good Lord gave mankind too much brain which has become destructive; a special brain in producing products to create a pollution of the planet not to last even the next hundred years. Can you imagine? The planet probably will not survive man's smartness. There is irony in this. The kind of irony nature always hands out.

Now, I am trying to stretch things out. I am becoming stubborn about these events, my visitors not being invited, still they arrive and asking me to trip with them. So, I tell them, much as I would like to leave this very minute, we will need to wait for the dog to do its business. She can't be left in the house all day by herself; none here to let her out should she need a bowel movement. We will wait.

This really begins to anger the entourage, Valerie saying she has never heard of something so foolish, holding up an excursion, a trip to Grimsby to waiting grandchildren, held up, the whole bunch, waiting for a dog to squeeze a stool.

But I insist, to make the wait more endurable, offering them some cookies, promising them a hot chocolate, I have some of the Dutch type, very smooth and I would be glad to put it into preparation. Just say the word.

An hour is spent, the three of us peering out the back glass slider door, our eyes on my dog Sue as she sniffs around. Finally she makes a deposit and everyone gives a sigh of relief. Except me. I have run out of excuses. Time to go.

We load into the van. Me, placed in the back passenger seat. Soon we are out of town and headed down superhighway 401 to Grimsby. All the conversation is very up, everybody remarking on how soon there will be new foliage, this being spring and all. Everything okey dokey.

Now terrible things begin to happen. I suddenly hear someone say *retirement home*. And then directly I am told, in Grimsby there is a very lovely retirement home, a home of a welcoming staff, a friendly physician, and plenty of activities. A life far better than the one I had been living, no longer just sitting on the couch, day and night.

That sets me off.

I am not ashamed to say I became violent. There is a time when violence is required. Just not to sit and take it from others, but protest, and here they have tricked me! They know I would not have gotten into their damned van if they said, hey hurry up, get dressed, let's go to a retirement home; where each day runs into the other, time lost in a fog, medicaments pushed down your throat like clockwork, eating things of the cafeteria, nothing Hungarian, but foods of a blandness, made to offend no one, pleasing none in the outcome. These three, arriving unannounced on my doorstep, if they had said these confining things at the outset, do you think I would have gotten into their damned van?

Not at all.

And where is the dutiful son through all of this? Why didn't he show up with these three betrayers? Was he too scared? Was that him, his grey car parked down the street watching the action? This selfsame son, with whom for fifteen years I spent time daily, having chicken dinners, later to take a walk in a green park, is now staying away when I would need him the most?

All betrayers. Christ had them too. Not that I am as Christ, no not at all, I would never even suggest that I am, but the betrayers have always been with us. Christ had His. I've got mine. And I was a betrayer too; I need to admit to myself, betraying my husband John in his cancer, at long last agreeing to have the doctors ship him off for extended care, knowing he was near his end, him wanting to stay in his bed with the burnished headboard, his bed for a half a century. So now I am going to be served up the same.

And these people did not consult. Me giving Valerie that big welcoming hug, and now here she is, her mouth moving rapidly in front of me coming out with words like *retirement home* and how good it can be. Those are threatening words. Call it a retirement home all you want. It's an old age home in simple language, where all things done in this life comes to zero. Things like fearlessly crossing the stormy Atlantic on the *Belvedere*, surviving the loss of a father at an early age, marrying not for love but improvements, giving birth, taking care of others, these things account for nothing in a retirement home. No one knows you for these things in those places. Just a stopping off place before the graveyard. Not for me thank you. It might be okay for some, for those who like to be served perhaps, but not for those of an independent spirit.

But that is the best place they will say, for those with oncoming Alzheimer's. Could I recall all these things if I had the deadly

Alzheimer's? Sometimes my memory *is* bad, but only on certain days. Other days clear as crystals. I am deeply depressed, that's all. Old age brings on depression, regretful of the passage of time. That's it. Just depressed, and when young people are depressed, do they call that one Alzheimer's? Oh no, not at all. But when old people become depressed suddenly it's Alzheimer's. Surely, on some days I am very forgetful. But when young people are forgetful, it is said that they are just too busy, they are tired from business or something. But then, when old people are forgetful, here comes that damned Alzheimer's conclusive again.

Riding in this van now I become fearful. The voices are becoming muffled, my body cannot leave but my mind starts to escape. I cannot believe the events unfolding. I feel claustrophobic in this van, rushing at a high speed to a retirement home.

I swat Valerie. Just swat her several times, she now putting her arms up around her face, defending herself against my anger. And I am screaming accusations at her. Well, wouldn't you? I'm sure you would. People taking over your life. Accusing you of misremembering, the word Alzheimer's popping up regularly.

Stop this van! Stop it right here! Stop it on the superhighway! Stop it in this speedy traffic! I don't give a damn about the traffic!

"I will choke you Valerie, damn you. And you, you, the other two, you betrayers. I will choke you too. You bastards!

You goddamn bastards."

Can you see? I even screamed God's name in vain here in the van. Here I am, screaming this word for the very first time in my life. Never would I do this before this torment pushed on me today. Never did I use God's name in vain.

But I have been pushed into it. Now things really become violent with Valerie pushing me down into the seat, trying to sit on me, avoiding my swings. And I start to hyperventilate. Well, wouldn't you? All this uninvited violence taking place, and I guess my older son and his wife never witnessing hyperventilation before believe I am having a heart attack. The screaming van approaches Hamilton, and the McMaster Hospital on the route, which the van turns into, the occupants yelling for a doctor, or nurse, or orderly, *someone* to put me on a stretcher and get me into emergency.

This they do.

But by the time I regain my full capabilities, I notice they are all gone. I have scared them away. They leave me at the hospital abandoning any further trip to the *retirement home*.

Hooray! They have gone.

Now starts the questioning by the staff. Who are you, they ask? What is your name?

How did you get here? Where are you from? I become the mystery woman at the emergency ward, an interloper, arriving unescorted. No health insurance card. No identification. No answering of questions since I am now entering one of my confused states, remembering nothing, the mind a blank, except for the name of my doctor. I remember who he is. And I tell them it is Dr. Coe.

They must have a list of all the doctors in the country. Because, sure enough, my dutiful son arrives, Dr. Coe's office getting in touch with him, I would suppose.

Well, they must have told him, because coming through the door now is my son Johnnie from Waterloo, and I am coyly dressing myself as he comes in but cannot find my shoes. Did I come shoeless? I don't think so. I would never travel without shoes. I have an interest in shoes, my father having been a cobbler and a poet. So I would never leave without shoes, but here I am, shoeless.

"Johnnie, did you see my shoes?" This is the first thing I ask of my son, not even hello, how are you, have you come to visit or whatever, just where are my shoes? "Do you have them? Who has them? Someone has my shoes."

Now some kind of negotiations begin. My dutiful son is having a conversation with the ward doctor, heads bobbing up and down, hands giving out expressions, much conversation in progress. Soon, my son comes to me and says it is time to leave, where are your shoes? This is the selfsame question I having been asking of him, and why does he not hold some sort of search for my shoes instead of just an extended conversation with the ward doctor. So, I tell him I will not leave until my shoes are found, they are my favourite pair and I have a need of them. Off he goes now, a full search of the ward taking place, him interviewing the others in the emergency. After some time of this, he finally returns with a pair of paper slippers as replacement for my good shoes. For reasons I cannot explain, I accept the paper slippers, offering no argument, place them on my feet and prepare to leave the hospital, just one more event.

WE ARE WALKING ACROSS THE PARKING LOT, ME in my paper slippers, my son having me by the hand, headed toward the car. As we start driving, a party atmosphere begins like in the old days, we are each happy, me laughing, my son laughing, his wife too, everyone in a good mood, isn't this a great day? Isn't everything wonderful? There is a continuous party atmosphere, my son throwing in humour, me throwing in my nickel's worth, his wife, hers, a full hour and a half of merriment, just like old times.

I am returning to Belmont Avenue, to my cottage and I am getting my life back again. That's what I believe.

After one hour of driving time, they stop the car at a large building not seen to me, before. There is a yellow bus in front, stopped, the yellow school bus type, and there are old people, many are feeble, wheelchairs abound, the livelier ones skilling their way around, positioning themselves to the front door, and the rest of them waiting for a pusher. I say to my son,

"What's this? What's going on?" My son says, "Congratulations, Mother, this is your new home."

That's all I can remember for a few minutes. My mind has escaped, unable to take in. I am silent, the tears are building up, and I begin to weep silently with the feeling of doom. I begin to realize what is going on. I look down unto my hands on my lap, avoiding the image before me. Wishing it away. The wish not granted.

I am learning what hypocrites my children are. How unfaithful. I served my family. I cared for them to the fullest, made my kitchen, kissed their hurts, put myself second. If my child needs ice skates, I delay my winter coat. If my child needs a bike, I will get one somehow, too. This has always been my rule of conduct where my children were concerned. And this is the reward.

Yes surely, I am now into my nineties and I am troublesome. And yes, I have serious clinical depression, if not full blown Alzheimer's. I am not an easy one.

And now I see, my children cannot deal with an old woman's depression, sending her to paid keepers. Not every family would do as such. The Old Order Mennonites to give an example, having a difficult oldster to care for, they just build another room onto the family home, putting her chattels in there, and she earns her keep with the chickens, collecting eggs, making a purpose for herself, not as in modern life, the government providing money for huge new buildings, chrome and glass and brick becoming permanent housing for the oldsters, swifting away the purpose in life.

Well, this is not for me. Not for me this old age home, pills in distribution by dutiful nurses, the nurse saying take them, just take them, I have others to look after, don't doddle. So much better for the Old Order Mennonite old women, collecting the eggs even if tetchy about it.

And I am thinking: if they put me in here, what will become of my chattels? My furniture, the tea wagon with the big wheels, and the knick-knacks I have collected over the years, souvenirs of other places, the fine fabrics I have carefully placed away. The linens of the finest quality I have collected, too good to put out in use, just intended to be viewed for their beauty, hand stitched of a European pattern. All my good things that I have loved for a lifetime. What will happen to my Stromberg-Carlson mantle radio I have used for fifty years, always giving reliable service, never failing me, where will it go? My husband once made fun of me for collecting knick-knacks; made sport of me for these collections, but I love each little figurine with a passion, little oriental ladies, fan in hand, and always presenting a pretty smile. My knick-knacks, bric-a-brac, curios, gewgaws and trinkets, call them what you will, I loved them all, I appreciated them and I made them important to me. What will become of these things of little value to others, but of great value to me? What?

And my other prizes, my dog and my cat who are at home this very moment in my cottage on Belmont Avenue a hundred miles from here. My dog is old, no chance for her for adoption, or my cat of eleven years, who will want her? They will needle both. Both so valued by me, so loved by me, to be discarded now by people who don't know the fullest value of these two animals, their character, their real value, not in their appearance, the dog is twice too plain by any estimate, her coat gone old, giving a reduced appearance. But I know these two creatures as living things and their personalities are part of my life.

The yellow bus of the old and infirm, slowly unload before my very eyes. Is this what is waiting for me? Is this where I end up, and worse, brought here by my children.

I hear again the words, "Mother, this is your new home."

I scream at him.

Sitting on the passenger side, I am beating my hands on the dashboard of his car until he stops me from doing such saying I will break my hands. But I keep beating, yelling at my son,

"Look at these people getting off this yellow bus. Look at them! Is this me? Am I as this? This is not my condition. I am strong in body. I am depressed yes. I know I am. I feel out of myself. But I am not in this kind of weakened condition, to need living help. You have betrayed me! My own sons, the ones I gave life to, have betrayed me! Have lied to me. Have tricked me. I despise dishonesty in all its many forms. How can this happen! Retirement home? What the hell are you talking about? I *am* in retirement on Belmont Avenue, do you not understand? That's where I am in retirement. With my dog and my cat, I am in retirement. Collecting pebbles. Keeping my garden. What you are doing to me is dreadful. I do not deserve this as an outcome. It is wrong. Improper."

I scream.

My screaming and my disappointment brings on hyperventilation, getting too much oxygen in the blood to the brain, threatening an unconsciousness state.

And I pass out. I go unconscious. Next thing I know, I awake in a room I have not seen before, the sons staring down at me, a room of permanence *in a home for the aged*. This awful realization comes to me. I know now what will happen. I will be here now for my remaining days. All my human efforts, every kindness extended, every thing accomplished, every effort made, adds up to zero.

* * *

IN THE MONTHS AND YEARS TO FOLLOW IN THIS PLACE, I WILL begin now to play a strange game. At the retirement home, where the staff is truly kind and caring, always trying to appear interested, even if not, I am asked in a casual way about my beautiful English cottage on Belmont, I feign ignorance. When asked of my animal pets, my dog and my cat, I pretend not to know, not even to ask what was their fate and are they deceased. These two creatures with which I spent each day for a dozen years, the final days of my independence, I pretend not to care of. But when the nurse leaves my room, I squeeze out the tears.

Nor would I ask of my sons with their visits, what is the final fate of my bric-a-brac from my house? The gewgaws and trinkets. What happened? Where did they go? Where are they now? The little carved oriental lady figurine, she with the parasol shielding herself from the sun. Where is she now, once a part of my daily life, perhaps now swifted away to another's mantle.

These were my precious things. Not precious in cash value, but precious as pieces of my life's history. I have been put away, my time wasted, my life dripping away a day at a time, each day more alike than the one before.

But time changes the outlook. Time passes and I have forgiven my betrayers. And when my son and his wife come to visit, they walk me outdoors to the back of the building, to the little vest pocket park out there, and in the warming sun of the late spring morning, we seat ourselves, my son on one side, his wife on the other, and I will take each of their hands, clasped palm to palm in mine, and sitting side by side, I will squeeze their hands against my body, squeeze ever so hard, and close my eyes with my face to the sun, and there is an amount of contentment in this.

Some days I deny the betrayal even happened, gaming myself, telling myself that I put my ownself in here, like doing such was of my own choosing. I seem to need to make up this story, perhaps to preserve my love for my children, pretending like they would never do this to me. In my mind of minds, it never happened. I game it away. ❦

Post Script

AS THIS TALE IS WRITTEN, ZARAH PETRI IS NINETY-SIX YEARS old. Her daily routine is simple: each morning at about ten, she is taken down to the crafts room where she sits knitting the same afghan she began when she first arrived here, years ago.

Speaking to no one in particular, she purses her lips and announces in a bittersweet way,

> Someday this afghan will be finished and when it is, I will pass it along to my dutiful son, the one who took me to the city of Waterloo, where I lived for fifteen years with my dog and my cat; where I weeded my garden, and collected my pebbles which suddenly ended, when I was whisked away. I will gift him with this simple afghan.
> And then he will be fully repaid.

Afterword

We would like to thank the staff of nurses and all other caregivers at Albright Manor for every kindness extended to our mother. In truth, they gave to Zarah the attention and personal care her family could not. She would say, "One mother gives care to three sons; three sons cannot give care to one mother."

And that still troubles us.

Reader Reviews to: letterbox222@gmail.com